The American Institute of Architects Press
1735 New York Avenue N.W., Washington, D.C. 20006
©1988 by the American Institute of Architects
All rights reserved. Printed in the United States.

ISBN #1-55835-002-0

# THE CREATION OF SHELTER

BY NORA RICHTER GREER

THE AMERICAN INSTITUTE OF ARCHITECTS PRESS
WASHINGTON, D.C., 1988

# CONTENTS

*To be homeless is a condition most of us even fear to imagine—let alone experience. And, too often, fear inhibits action. In contrast, the 29 Search for Shelter projects documented in this book reflect the united effort of dedicated men and women who care deeply about the far-too-many homeless Americans who walk among us; architects and others have banded together to form Search for Shelter groups to help the homeless in their communities. Local communities finding local solutions is what makes this program work. But government has a role, as well. Federal funding from the Stewart B. McKinney Act is helping turn some of the designs seen here into reality. But many are still on the drawing board. A commitment to a stronger national housing policy, encouragement of public/private partnerships to develop low-cost housing, and the dedication of men and women at the local level are all needed. Americans cannot just fear homelessness, we must work together, architects and others, to prevent it. We, as a nation, must renew our commitment to the 1949 Housing Act which declared as national policy the goal of "a decent home and suitable living environment for every American family."*

Ted Pappas, FAIA, President
American Institute of Architects

*The the Search for Shelter program has become an opportunity for educators, students, architects, and others to enact change. As a result, architecture students have grown keenly aware of the important role that they will assume in creating livable cities that shelter the underprivileged members of our society. As the architects of our future, these students have proudly displayed to their communities and their profession the commitment to resolving the housing crisis.*

*During the past year, hundreds of architecture students devoted thousands of hours to serve as active members of the Search for Shelter design charette teams. From Dallas to Minneapolis, San Francisco to Boston, architecture students challenged local communities to address and respond to this crisis and came away rewarded for their efforts. Students today believe the time is ripe for design, construction, and housing professionals to bring their services to bear on easing the plight of the homeless and other populations at risk. The American Institute of Architecture Students, Inc., is proud to play a key role in the realization of these new housing opportunities.*

Matthew W. Gilbertson, President
American Institute of Architecture Students

*Joining the NeighborWorks network with the American Institute of Architects and the American Institute of Architecture Students has made for a fruitful partnership. Through the Search for Shelter, we are learning how to build the necessary community resolve to make permanent inroads into solving the problem of homelessness. Matching homeless families with vacant properties is not only cost-effective, it solves two problems at once. A homeless family finds a home, and a vacant property's blighting influence is removed from a neighborhood. In partnership with the architectural fraternity, NeighborWorks organizations serving over 300 neighborhoods throughout America are learning how their neighborhood revitalization partnerships can be part of a citizen-based effort to free our nation of the shame of Americans homeless in the most prosperous nation on earth.*

William A. Whiteside, Executive Director
Neighborhood Reinvestment Corporation

# FOREWORD

6

In 1984 the AIA Housing Committee out of curiosity began to take note of the homeless. We noticed an increasing number of people who were excluded from even basic housing, and wondered who they were and why they didn't have homes. As we learned more we found that this nation's housing delivery system is not as simple as it appears. Because of its intricacy, those at the margins of society were losing out to higher economic uses of urban land.

We were startled to acknowledge our role in that unfairness. As architects, we advocate for urban renewal and community revitalization, but we found that those "improvements" have resulted in the destruction of whole neighborhoods. We urged the replacement of urban slums with bright new housing complexes, but often created institutional, high-rise superghettos. We watched residential hotels knocked down to make room for gleaming office and commercial buildings—with no provision for those displaced.

Now we seek solutions to remedy those mistakes. We are looking for the means to provide temporary, humane shelter—crisis intervention for the homeless; transitional housing that offers support and stabilization for disrupted lives; and creative, long-term housing solutions. We seek housing as an integral part of a continuum of basic human needs—a decent home in a suitable living environment, with personal and family supports, health care, and job training.

We have deepened our commitment to address those needs. The AIA Housing Committee has taken a leadership role in developing the Search for Shelter program; the first of a series of workshops were held around the country in 1987. We have formed a partnership with the American Institute of Architecture Students and Neighborhood Reinvestment Corporation to reach out to new communities and other professionals in our quest for solutions to the housing crisis.

This book presents solutions from those first workshops. In the variety of directions taken by different groups, each response illuminates a specific perception of the housing crisis. Community focus has been the source of the Search for Shelter's success—a process predicated on a broad participation of diverse community members asking difficult questions early in a project and placing trust in an interactive dialogue focusing on homelessness as a community concern.

The empowerment of prospective tenants in that process has been crucial, encouraging future residents to share responsibility and authority in the development of projects. New bonds of ownership, identity, and self-reliance have been as much the product of these solutions as the housing itself. In the workshops, we have witnessed the breaking down of the "not-in-my-backyard" barriers of neighborhood and community resistance and the acknowledgment that those without homes do deserve decent housing and a place in the community.

There is much work left to do to understand homelessness and its relationship to the much broader low-income housing crisis that exists. Ultimately, homelessness cannot be separated from the issue of justice for all—from a more equitable sharing in the nation's economy, from our commitment to social, political, and cultural inclusion in our society, and to the elimination of racial and ethnic prejudice. Those should be added to the federal Congressional debate over if and how this nation's 1949 commitment to "a decent home and a suitable living environment for all" should and can be met. In this diverse and rich nation, the housing crisis is not an issue of resources; it is a matter of national will.

*The Creation of Shelter* offers a close look at the unique responses of the first Search for Shelter workshops. The solutions come not from academic, theoretical planning, but from the pragmatic experience of coalitions coming together for a brief moment, sharing perceptions and wills to hammer out solutions to most unique community needs.

We are pleased to share their vision and solutions to assist you in your own journey of creation.

D. Blake Chambliss, FAIA
Anderson Mason Dale P.C.
Denver, Colo.   7

# PREFACE

8

Amid the architecture of riches in this country, there is an architecture of fear and abandonment, of isolation and deprivation, where lost souls barely survive from day to day. It is an architecture that many refuse to acknowledge, yet the list of potential occupants grows daily. This architecture of neglect symbolizes our "great" society's failing—its inability to feel compassion for the weakest among us.

Picture this: It was a rainy fall day in New York City, the kind that nudges at the bones; the occasion, an official tour of city shelters for visitors from Washington, D.C. The last stop was the Fort Washington armory in upper Manhattan. Those of us visiting that day knew of this shelter through menacing tales of 1,000 army surplus cots lined up in tight rows on the armory gymnasium floor, a place never quiet, never still, until the shelter guests are put out on the streets the next morning.

Somehow, though, descriptions of shelters never prepares one for the reality. In the case of Fort Washington the reality was much worse than any of us had thought possible.

We entered the shelter to find hordes of men in the armory's lobby—a cavernous space lit by the glare of two bare bulbs hanging from the ceiling. Shuffling around in the lobby were the shelter guests waiting to be let in for the evening. Among the sea of faces were men of different creeds and nationalities, the young and old, the seemingly able-bodied and handicapped. Fully comprehending their suffering was more than any of us could do. In retrospect it seems a musty image flashed across a black-and-white television screen. Yet we all quietly knew we were glimpsing a slice of our society's underworld—and those men were society's untouchables.

After a short while, we were led into the armory's gymnasium—once again, the mind, not quite able to absorb the scene, filtered it through the black-and-white t.v. When the reality hit, we turned around as if by some brute force, unable to penetrate the room any further. Without saying anything, we knew what our collective thoughts were—it was terrifying and inhumane. Surely it was the aftermath of a hor-

9

rible natural disaster rather than representative of the way America cares for the weakest among us.

For the homeless in this country, conditions are bad; the homeless survive in environments more dreadful than prison inmates do, a comment perhaps on a nation's twisted morality. And while temporary shelter can be found in much more benevolent forms than Fort Washington, it remains just that—temporary. What is needed is more decent, low-cost housing—places for people to call home for extended periods of time, where an individual or a family can then put a broken life back together again.

Seeking that housing raises a slew of questions: What is this housing crisis that has caused dislocation for so many Americans? Can it be solved? Who will build and manage the housing? Where will that housing be located? What form will it take? Do we need to lower housing standards to lower costs? Should housing costs be subsidized and by whom? What role should government—local, state, or federal—assume? What about the private sector? Does the nation care enough to find solutions to the crisis?

The search for answers is a personal quest, as is whether, or how, one could be actively involved. Yet, it is also a more universal pursuit, for solace can be found in the swelling numbers of Americans commiting time, energy, and caring toward easing the crisis. During the past decade that circle has widened from the traditional care givers—the Salvation Army shelters, the Rescue Missions—to city and state governments, who have reshaped their housing programs both for temporary and longer-term users and have found creative ways to finance the new endeavors. Large and small nonprofit housing groups have formed to begin to piece together a new environment for the less well-off in our nation. Experts in professions relating to homelessness and housing, including those in the social services arena, have protested more vehemently with each passing year.

These people are responding to a drastic change in the housing system for the poor in this country.

As the federal government and the private development market has stepped back, these others have come forward. Yet, all now know the crisis can not end without the resources of the federal government. Most fear that the predicted widening of the crisis will all too soon become a reality.

*The Creation of Shelter* was written for three purposes: to further protest the living conditions in this country for the homeless and those with little means; to celebrate the grassroots' response to the housing crisis; and to broaden the dialogue on what is appropriate, decent, affordable, long-term housing for the poorest in our country. *The Creation of Shelter* will be considered a success if it solicits as many questions as it answers.

A large portion of *The Creation of Shelter* is devoted to the Search for Shelter program, a joint effort between the American Institute of Architects, the American Institute of Architecture Students, and Neighborhood Reinvestment. As recorded here, the results of that effort to bring architects, architecture students, housing experts, government officials, service providers, and others together to design shelters or learn more about shelter design are tremendous. The Search for Shelter was created by a small group of AIA staff who wondered why architects weren't more concerned and vocal about the housing crisis. The program's results suggest that many just didn't know how to offer help in a meaningful way. We have been pleased to light the way.

Nora Richter Greer
Senior Editor, *Architecture*
Author, *The Search for Shelter*

Special thanks to my husband William for his patience and love, to the McKnew-Thomas clan for its guidance, to the Search for Shelter crew members for their support, and to the creative people who helped me put *The Creation of Shelter* together.

ACKNOWLEDGMENTS

Copy editor: Vicki Venker
Cover photo © Shephard Sherbell, Picture Group
Editor: Gretchen Smith Mui
Graphic consultant: Carole Palmer
Graphic designer: Kathleen Vetter
Typesetting: Hodges Typographers,
   Silver Spring, Md.

*The Creation of Shelter* was made possible through
the support of the AIA Press, *Architecture,* and
the Search for Shelter program sponsors—the
American Institute of Architects (AIA), the
American Institute of Architecture Students (AIAS),
and Neighborhood Reinvestment Corporation.

The American Institute of Architects
   The AIA Housing Committee
   D. Blake Chambliss, FAIA
   Lee Waldrep
   Ravi Waldon, AIA
   Laurie Anderson
   Nora Richter Greer
   Paul Knapp
   Anne Howell
   Margorie Valin

The American Institute of Architecture Students
   Carl Costello
   Kent Davidson
   Karen Cordes
   Matt Gilbertson
   Irene Dumas

Neighborhood Reinvestment
   Jane Milner
   Steve Allen

Contributors to the Search for Shelter
   Council of State Housing Agencies
   International Conference of Building Officials

The poem by MKW III on page 89 entitled
"Mantra" was reproduced from *Forgotten Voices/Unfor-
gettable Dreams,* with permission of the National Coalition for the Homeless, Deborah Mashibini, editor.

# CASE STUDIES

12

Above all else, *The Creation of Shelter* celebrates just that—the efforts of people across the country who are striving to create housing for the homeless and other victims of the current housing crisis. Following are the early results of the tremendous response to the crisis from architects, architecture students, educators, housing experts, shelter and social service providers, community leaders, and others through "The Search for Shelter."

No two case studies are alike, for each Search for Shelter team thoughtfully responded to the particular housing problems in its own community. Universal, however, is the need to create housing—emergency, transitional, or long-term—that offers a sense of privacy to its occupants, encourages communal activities, and is domestic in scale, materials, and form. The emphasis is on home rather than institution. Given the typical tight construction and operating budgets, fulfilling these requirements is no easy task.

The majority of the Search for Shelter teams chose to design shelters for the homeless and long-term, low-cost housing by renovating existing buildings: the more traditional housing types (former group homes, residential hotels, and row houses), but also less familiar ones (schools, motels, nursing homes, churches, and warehouses).

Each team decided the scope of its project—whether it would be simply an investigation of housing for the homeless or those with little means or if an actual shelter would result. Now, a year after the first 29 Search for Shelter workshops (the work from Miami and Cincinnati is not seen here), 19 projects are to be built. Some of these projects might have occurred without the Search for Shelter, yet each one will be a more welcoming environment because of it. Just as importantly, new alliances in communities have been formed; a few will likely grow into longer-term partnerships. And a method for rallying a community has brought successes far beyond what was thought possible. The dialogue on housing the homeless and those with little means has been significantly expanded.

# PHOENIX, ARIZONA

Since 1970 Phoenix has lost the majority of its single-room-occupancy (SRO) units. Thirty-two of the 36 SRO hotels downtown have been demolished, rehabilitated for other uses, abandoned, or subject to arson. The high number of units lost— 1,400—has significantly contributed to the rise in homelessness in Phoenix and its surrounds: In Maricopa County, the estimated number of homeless persons is 6,000.

As attention across the country has begun to focus on easing the plight of the homeless, the SRO is seen as an extremely viable housing type. In Phoenix the potential contribution of SROs and possible locations of such buildings are being examined. Can SROs provide adequate environments for their residents and at the same time not hinder a downtown revival? Participation in this debate was the intent behind the Phoenix Search for Shelter workshop.

Under close scrutiny is the concept of small shelters dispersed throughout the city. Advocates argue that smaller shelters are more humane than larger ones. By being spread throughout a city, the advocates maintain, each shelter would likely be better received in its immediate neighborhood.

The Phoenix Search for Shelter task force chose for its workshop three buildings to be renovated into SROs: (1) a vacant nursing home in a residential neighborhood; (2) an aging, centrally located motel; (3) and a warehouse complex located at the periphery of a newly reviving part of downtown.

The nursing home would be renovated into an SRO for 31 single women. The need for such an SRO is clearly evident: Approximately 1,000 women have stayed in the city's emergency shelter during the past year. But several questions must be resolved: What are the special environmental needs of low-income, formerly homeless women? How can the SRO fit into the residential setting? What services and amenities need to be provided on site?

Of utmost importance to the two design teams was changing the institutional ambience of the 16,500-square-foot nursing home into a more domestic one. Also needed were communal areas to serve as "living rooms" for the bedrooms. Creating a secure environment for the guests also was important.

To soften the building's exterior, both design solutions call for the addition of a front porch. They also suggest turning the outdoor courtyard at the heart of the building into a social gathering place. One team seeks to create a sense of place and individuality by designing an interior street—each room would have a unique entrance and the color scheme in the halls would vary.

The design solutions also call for the incorporation on the site of small, prefabricated "houses" donated by a local military base. The open area surrounding these units and the nursing home would become a neighborhood park.

No social services would be available on site; however, the residential manager could refer tenants to appropriate care providers in the community. The former nursing home is near a major bus route. On-site amenities would include interior gathering spaces, maid service, laundry facilities, and a kitchen.

These workshop design solutions will be taken into account when the build-

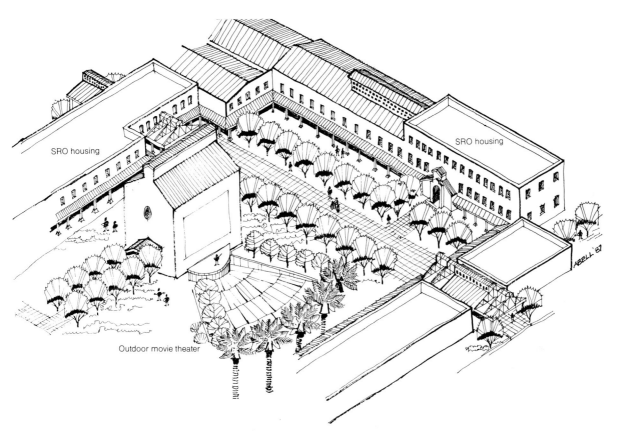

SRO housing

SRO housing

Outdoor movie theater

ABELL '87

ing is rehabilitated by the Community Housing Partnership. A nonprofit housing corporation, the partnership will acquire the building through a conventional loan guaranteed by Valley Partnership, a group of local developers. Funding has also been requested from HUD under the SRO Moderate Rehabilitation Program established by the Stewart B. McKinney Homeless Assistance Act of 1987. Acquisition costs are estimated at $500,000 and rehabilitation costs at $300,000.

In the case of the motel, the design problem is to create a pleasant, hospitable environment for residents in a downtown setting. At issue is whether this building type can be adequately adapted as an SRO.

The specific populations chosen for this SRO would be young men just entering the job market and retired men. Both groups are likely to benefit from this permanent, low-cost housing. As in the nursing home redesign, there would be no social services on the site. The design efforts therefore focused on creating pleasant private and communal environments.

To change the sterile atmosphere of the 1950s motel into a homelike environment, the design team created a hierarchy of private and public spaces, thus promoting different types of social interaction. The opportunity for each guest to personalize his room was stressed. Envisioned are 45 rooms plus the manager's quarters.

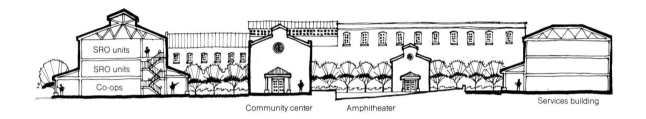

SRO units
SRO units
Co-ops

Community center    Amphitheater    Services building

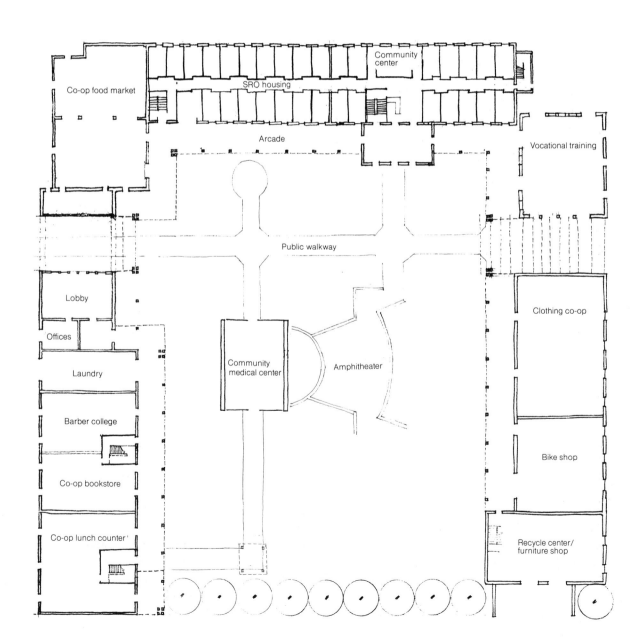

Co-op food market

SRO housing

Community center

Arcade

Vocational training

Public walkway

Lobby

Offices

Laundry

Barber college

Co-op bookstore

Co-op lunch counter

Community medical center

Amphitheater

Clothing co-op

Bike shop

Recycle center/ furniture shop

The Community Housing Partnership plans to purchase the motel with a loan from the Valley Partnership and a HUD grant. The motel, however, is second in priority to the nursing home conversion. Acquisition costs are estimated at $500,000 and rehabilitation costs at $100,000.

In the warehouse project, an SRO would be created two blocks south of the downtown redevelopment district. Pertinent questions include the following: Would the SRO be compatible with the neighboring retail and restaurant establishments? How can the design enhance the downtown development? Can such a facility be designed to adequately meet the needs of all potential residents?

Again, no social services would be provided on the site, but could be obtained nearby. Instead, the two design teams working on this project incorporated into the design restaurants and shops, which could be used by the SRO residents and could also provide income for the SRO's upkeep. One team even calls for a cooperative to supply clothing, food, barber shop, and other services to the residents.

The warehouse chosen for the workshop is currently used by a state public utility company. Although it is not for sale, it was selected as an example of the warehouses that could be redesigned for low-income housing. The condition of buildings in the warehouse district ranges from excellent to dilapidated. Within the warehouse would be created 100 to 150 single-room-occupancy units, if renovation occurs in the future.

*Postscript.* In early December 1987, the Community Housing Partnership learned that it would receive $1 million in HUD funding over the next 10 years to rehabilitate the vacant nursing home into permanent housing for homeless single women. HUD will also provide Section 8 certificates for the 31 SRO residents. Fred Karnas, CHP executive director, said, "The AIA charrette played a key role in the success of the CHP and City of Phoenix Neighborhood Improvement and Housing Department proposal to HUD. The drawings created by the charrette teams brought the project to life for HUD and for local backers, including banks and developers."

CONTACT
Fred Karnas
Executive Director
Community Housing Partnership
P.O. Box 25312
Phoenix, Ariz. 85002
(602) 942-2349

SPONSORS & PARTICIPANTS
Arizona Society of Architects/AIA
Arizona State University, College of Architecture and Environmental Design
Arizona State University Chapter AIAS
Central Arizona Chapter/AIA
Communities by Design
Community Housing Partnership
Junior League of Phoenix, Task Force on the Homeless
NHS of Phoenix, Inc.
Neighborhood Improvement and Housing Department, City of Phoenix
Phoenix Community Alliance
Rio Salado Chapter/AIA
Valley Partnership

# LOS ANGELES, CALIFORNIA

Among the estimated 30,000 to 35,000 homeless persons in Los Angeles, the group most in need of assistance is families with children, who now roam the streets, live in cars or tents, or occupy squats (abandoned, dilapidated housing). To address the particular needs of homeless families, the Los Angeles Chapter/AIA organized a Search for Shelter competition. A village that incorporates many of the ideas generated by the competition may actually be built in the future.

The competition's focus was designing a new village for 64 persons on a 30,000-square-foot lot. The accommodations need to be flexible enough to house, over time, families of various sizes.

Additional programmatic requirements included the following:
• a minimum room size of 120 square feet;
• an "upbeat," wholesome appearance;
• the use of any of the following building components — tents, trailers, domes, stacks, platforms, adaption of various manufactured items, city stock of modules, plywood and frame construction;
• a staff unit to house reception activities, referral services, and a message and mail center (staff should be able to observe entrances and public open spaces);
• community amenities such as a place for small group gatherings, a game area, barbecue pit, storage space, landscaped areas for quiet sitting and play, children's playground, bulletin board, and flag pole;
• individual or shared kitchen and bath facilities;
• parking for 27 cars, with three spaces reserved for the handicapped.

In all, 52 entries were received, from architects and students in California, Arizona, Texas, and Rhode Island. And while no single winner emerged, three projects were chosen for honor awards and six for merit awards.

Overall, the competition received mixed reviews. On the negative side, architects did not participate in large numbers. Most of the entries were from students. Task force chairman Pamela Edwards-Kammer explains: "The fees for shelters are so low that architects lose money on the jobs. Only those who are outrageously committed pursue them, even though there's an urgent problem."

Also, some of the competition jurors felt that the special needs of the homeless were not completely understood and that, in turn, the solutions were not sensitive enough to those needs. For example, some designers paid little attention to the village's security, even though homeless persons are highly sensitive to the safety of their immediate surroundings.

On the positive side, many participants called the project "invigorating" and said it raised the awareness of the architects, students, teachers, and the public to the issues surrounding one segment of the homeless population. As Gary Squier, coordinator of Los Angeles's efforts to increase affordable housing remarked, "The contest was valuable because it focused the attention of the academic community on the need for shelter."

Spurred on by the Search for Shelter efforts, architects in Los Angeles will continue to look for a potential site for a prototype village.

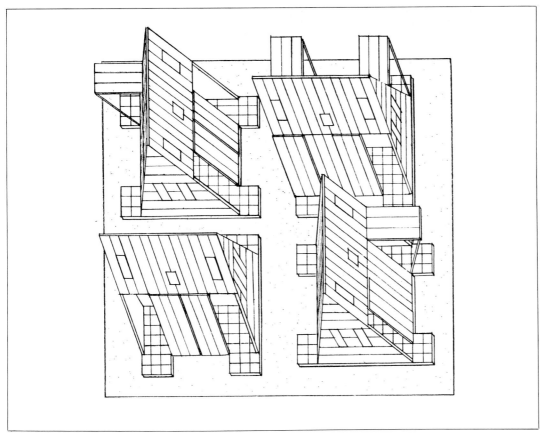

Design by Christa Froestl

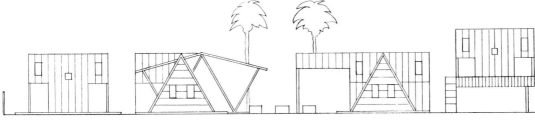

Demountable units for families

CONTACT
Pamela Edwards-Kammer
12304 Moorpark Street
Studio City, Calif. 91604
(818) 762-7874

COMPETITION WINNERS
Honor awards:
Melissa Eldridge, Southern California
    Institute of Architecture
Christa Froestl, Culver City, Calif.
Gerlinde Leiding and Yashuhiro
    Tomono, Austin, Tex.
Merit awards:
Ingrid Borgardf, Woodbury University
Dean Harris, Southern California Insti-
    tute of Architecture
George Nakatani and Lalida Pinsuvana
Karl Schurz, Southern California Insti-
    tute of Architecture

Michael Tarne, Southern California
    Institute of Architecture
Michael Whitby, Southern California
    Institute of Architecture

Jurors:
James R. Bonar, FAIA, Los Angeles
Pamela Edwards-Kammer, Studio City,
    Calif.
Richard Keating, FAIA, Los Angeles
John MacGuire, Community Develop-
    ment Agency, Los Angeles
John Mutlow, AIA, Los Angeles
Rob Wellington Quigley, AIA, San
    Diego
Johannes Van Tilberg, AIA, Santa
    Monica

SPONSOR
Los Angeles Chapter/AIA

# SAN MATEO COUNTY, CALIFORNIA

The estimated number of homeless in San Mateo County is 6,000 persons, with families comprising 60 percent of this population. And while some shelter and services are available, county officials and others seeking to aid the homeless lacked a clear picture of where the homeless are, who they are, what kind of shelter is available, what other needs they might have. It was the San Mateo County Search for Shelter team—architecture students from the College of San Mateo and professional advisor Morton Frank, AIA, with the help of the San Mateo Chapter/AIA—that developed the first comprehensive survey of the homeless in the county

Basically, the team's goal was to review "how public and private non-profit agencies within the county had been responding to the homeless problem and what was the general vision for the future," in the words of Frank. The team first reviewed all previous studies of the homeless in San Mateo. From this base of information members of the team conducted in-depth interviews with officials of the public and private organizations aiding the homeless.

The four existing shelters were visited, photographs were taken, and then measured drawings were produced. The drawings, photographs, and summaries of the data were compiled on illustration boards. With these in hand, the Search for Shelter team meet with the San Mateo County Housing Task Force and the San Mateo Board of Supervisors.

Three of the four shelters in the

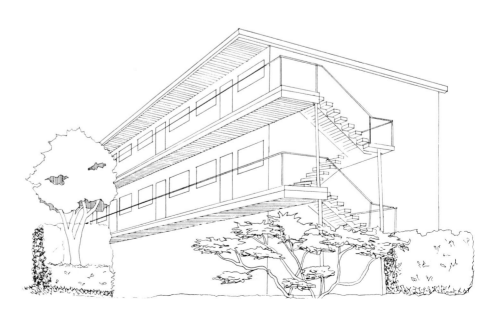

county were operated by the Family Living Centers organization. The Search for Shelter team was particularly impressed with this organization's goal of promoting a sense of stability and normalcy in a family's living arrangement, while at the same time providing more comprehensive services — counseling, workshops, referrals, and other services directed toward helping a family secure permanent housing and employment.

The results, Frank says, were impressive. "A solid coalition was formed consisting of public and private agencies together with the San Mateo Chapter/AIA and the College of San Mateo/AIAS Chapter for the purpose of going forward with a more inspired program that will now include an architectural involvement."

*The existing Redwood City Family Living Center promotes a sense of stability and normalcy in a family's living arrangement.*

CONTACT

Morton Frank, AIA
491 Seaport Court
Redwood City, Calif. 94063
(415) 369-6400

SPONSORS & PARTICIPANTS

College of San Mateo, School of Architecture
College of San Mateo Chapter/AIAS
Emergency Housing Consortium
Morton Frank, AIA, Workshop Professional Advisor
San Mateo Building Trades Council
San Mateo County Board of Supervisors
San Mateo County Chapter/AIA
San Mateo County Economic Development Association
San Mateo County Housing Task Force
The United Way, Mid-County Action Plan Housing Committee

Typical unit

0    5    10 FT

# BOULDER, COLORADO

A large proportion of the chronically mentally ill in Boulder County are inappropriately housed: They are living on the streets; in inadequate surroundings with parents, friends, or relatives; in substandard housing; or in medical facilities not suited to their needs. The Boulder Search for Shelter task force members chose to examine the housing of the chronically mentally ill because, in their words, this group "could be more influenced by the physical design" of their housing than other homeless groups.

In housing the chronically mentally ill—the schizophrenic or manic-depressive—a broad range of facilities is needed, ranging from institutions for maximum care to housing designed to allow complete integration into a community. A middle ground between these two is a shared residence with live-in supervisory staff.

In Boulder County, the demand for specialized housing for the chronically mentally ill far outweighs the supply. The chronically mentally ill who are housed are served by the following facilities, which were designed as a stepped system of housing:
• Cedar House, which provides short-term (five to 12 days) housing for 12 persons, 24-hour supervision, and a complete meal plan. All medication is monitored and administered by the residential supervisor. Because of the county's shortage of transitional and long-term housing with supervised care, however, the guests often become longer-term residents.
• University House, which is intended for short-term housing but in reality houses guests for years, rather than months. The staff monitor daily living skills, medication, and money and time management.
• Alpine I, which is a fourplex with two-bedroom units for the residents. The supervisor monitors medication, holds weekly group meetings, and is available in case of a crisis.
• Alpine II, which is connected to Alpine I and has three fourplexes with eight one-bedroom units. Alpine I's supervisor is responsible for the less demanding needs of Alpine II residents. Alpine II is considered the last step before private residence.
• Community Support System Team, which is located at Maslin House and which serves 70 chronically mentally ill persons who do not live in supervised accommodations. At Maslin House the full range of supervisory services are offered, as well as educational, recreational, and social activities.

In designing for the chronically mentally ill, it is essential to understand their special needs. The Boulder task group worked from these observations: "For people suffering from this illness, too many stimuli can be overwhelming. A place of retreat can be essential to people who are easily upset in an active environment. Sometimes even a simple task such as boiling an egg can be overwhelming. These people are frequently deserted by their friends, and thus feel rejected and isolated."

In setting out the design program, the Search for Shelter task force acknowledged other services, activities, and relationships as crucial: case management, counseling, support by family and friends, medication, recreation and socialization activities, vocational reha-

22

bilitation, and self-motivation. The task force determined that the new facility should fill the existing gap between the high-cost, highly staffed Cedar House and the more independent living situation provided by University House.

Ideally, housing for as many as 15 residents and one supervisor would be provided in two buildings, with 8 bedrooms in each building. Each building would also have two or three bathrooms, a kitchen, dining room, and a television and music room. Space for outdoor activities is considered important. A laundry is required, as well as space for private counseling. The site should be close to a shopping district and to Maslin House. The buildings' design should appear residential; compliance with building codes is a given.

A design for such housing will be further examined by an architectural design class at the University of Colorado, Boulder.

CONTACT
David L. Paulson, AIA
University of Colorado
Campus Box 314
Boulder, Colo. 80309
(303) 492-7711

SPONSORS & PARTICIPANTS
Boulder Council on Aging
Boulder County Housing Authority
Boulder Jaycees
Boulder Shelter
Blake Chambliss, FAIA
City of Boulder Housing Authority
Colorado North Chapter/AIA
Community Action Program

Erik Hartronft Architect
Josie Health, Boulder County Commissioner
Mental Health Center
Homer Page, Boulder City Council
Dennis Rezendes, Management-Financial Development Consultant
Safehouse
Marvin Sparn, AIA
Wendy Thoreson, AIA
Dick Tumpes, AIA
University of Colorado at Boulder, College of Environmental Design. Faculty: John Feinberg
University of Colorado at Boulder Chapter/AIAS

# DENVER, COLORADO

In cities of various sizes throughout Colorado the homeless are present—as many as 15,000 to 20,000 yearly throughout the state, according to one estimate. Because of the prevalence of the homeless problem, the Denver Search for Shelter task force assigned four teams to work with four existing service providers in four different locations.

Project Helping Hand provides shelter and support services in an old downtown Denver hotel slated for demolition. The 40,000-square-foot building sleeps 150 persons a night in 100 rooms and has an employment program, day care center, and clothing distribution center. To ensure continuation of services after the hotel's demolition, the owner sought a new building of similar size.

For the replacement facility, the Search for Shelter team found a nearby, 100,000-square-foot building and designed a variety of accommodations—from dormitories with bunk beds to two- or four-person rooms to single-room-occupancy units. The design calls for administrative offices, a kitchen and cafeteria, a lounge, and a storage area on the first floor. The second floor would have 56 beds arranged in dormitory style, and the third through seventh floors would each have 26 beds in various sleeping arrangements.

To the southeast, in Lamar, the manager of a shelter located in an old church and adjoining parsonage wanted to redesign and expand the number of beds. Basically, the Search for Shelter team transformed the bedrooms and recreation space on the first floor and the lower floor (3 to 4 feet above grade) into small one- or two-person rooms or family rooms. The first floor of the parsonage would contain the dining room and kitchen, and the lower floor would house the lounge. Berming around the building would soften the exterior and help keep water away from the building.

North of Denver, in Brighton, the House of Neighborly Services provides training, a food bank, clothing distribution, and child care in a 3,600-square-foot school. To expand its services the management chose three possibilities—to enlarge the schoolhouse, to relocate in a large warehouse, or to build a new facility on another site. The organization approached the Search for Shelter team for an answer to the question of how best to evaluate these options.

The Search for Shelter team devised 16 criteria, as follow:
- neighborhood location
- service location
- construction/renovation costs
- maintenance
- lease option
- building condition
- zoning
- available space
- flexibility
- expansion possibilities
- administrative space
- food bank
- clothing bank
- education
- playgrounds
- housing.

Each of the three possible shelter locations was analyzed as excellent, good, or poor in light of these criteria. The answers weighed heavily in favor of renovating the shelter's current building.

In Pueblo, the Search for Shelter team worked with a shelter housing 40 men to develop a gradual renovation plan to accommodate women and children also. The populations would be separated by two separate staircases—one connecting the ground floor (common room, lobby, and showers) with the third floor (for women) and the other staircase going only to the second floor (for men). The large garage would be converted into family units. Play areas and a community room would be built between the garage and the main building.

CONTACT
Blake Chambliss, FAIA
Anderson, Mason & Dale
1615 17th Street
Denver, Colo. 80202
(303) 294-9448

SPONSORS & PARTICIPANTS
Ron Abo & Associates
Anderson Mason & Dale
Artemis Designs
Colorado Coalition for the Homeless
Colorado Division of Housing
Colorado Housing Finance Authority
Neighborhood Reinvestment Corp.
Office of the Governor
John D. Reece & Associates
Service providers: Scott Howser, Larry Ilg, Julie Murphy, Rev. Jim Ragsdale, Ed Sbarbaro, Emil Tanner
University of Colorado at Denver, Center for Built Environment Studies and College of Design and Planning: Students—Susan Bardwell, Robert Hailey, Catherine Hansen, Wilbur James, Tim Katers. Faculty—Phil Gallegos, Bernie Johns
University of Colorado at Denver Chapter/AIAS

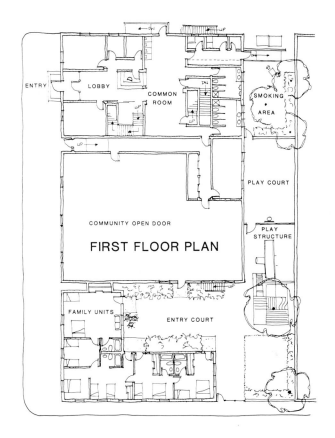

FIRST FLOOR PLAN

THIRD FLOOR PLAN
Posada Shelter, Pueblo

Stewart White

After an extensive examination of potential shelter needs, the D.C. Search for Shelter team choose to renovate a dilapidated, but potentially charming, row house in a residential neighborhood. When completed it would provide transitional housing for a dozen women; the house would be run by the local, non-profit organization Housing Opportunities for Women (HOW).

When that project is completed, the D.C. team will not disband; instead, the alliance of architects, architectural students, engineers, and construction companies will continue to work with shelter providers on a project-by-project basis offering their services either voluntarily or at cost.

In the HOW rowhouse each tenant and the resident manager will have a separate room and access to a large living room, bathrooms, and kitchen. Each floor will have a more intimate gathering space. Architecture students from Catholic University provided several different conceptual designs. The students then worked with the Weihe Partnership (and lead by architect Marc Nathanson) on the development of final plans. Overall, the house, which was once so rundown it could only be entered by a ladder to the second floor, will become a "fairly charming housing in a stable neighborhood," Nathanson said.

"An architecture tour de force this isn't and shouldn't be. It's a straight-forward, livable, economic facility. In a way, though, you work harder for a client like this—they just don't have the 'eye' that our commercial clients have," he added. The final design is highly sensitive to the users' needs and also successfully blends the once dilapted building back into the neighborhood.

This admirable contribution to housing homeless women in the District of Columbia may prove to be only the first of many collaborations between architects/builders/financiers and non-profit housing groups in the city. The Weihe Partnership and other Search for Shelter participants have set up an informal "clearinghouse" of professionals willing to turn their skills—on a volunteer or at-cost basis—to increasing the housing opportunities for the homeless in the city. In choosing the HOW project, a respository of other requests was created.

Besides the Wiehe partnership and the Catholic University students, others volunteering their services to refine the workshop results and to see the building through construction were Shefferman and Bigleson, construction engineers and JAK Construction Co.

CONTACT
Marc Nathanson
The Weihe Partnership
1666 K Street N.W.
Washington, D.C. 20006
(202) 857-8300

SPONSORS & PARTICIPANTS
ATEC Associates of Virginia
Add, Inc.
American Security Bank
Gordon Barnes
Biospherics, Inc.
Building Technology Inc.
Cathcart/Bonda, Inc.
Catholic University Chapter/AIAS
Catholic University, Department of
    Architecture and Planning
Computex Associates, Inc.
Consumers United Insurance Co.
The Design Corporation
The District of Columbia,
    Department of Housing and
    Community Development
HTB Inc.
Harris Design Group

Housing Opportunities for Women
    (HOW)
IMPACT, Inc.
JAK Construction, Inc.
Cynthia Johnston, AIA
Kemnitzer, Reid & Haffler, Architects
    Studios
The Kerns Group
Kress Cox Architects
La Morada Shelter
Life Management
McAuley Institute
Mother's House
National Cooperative Bank
PKP Engineers
W.G. Reed Architects
Rowley-Scher
Shefferman & Bigelson
Alan Sparber & Associates
Rev. John Steinbruck
Stohlman, Beuchert, Egan & Smith
Turner Associates Architects
Washington Chapter/AIA
The Weber Team
The Weihe Partnership

# GAINESVILLE, FLORIDA

No precise count had been made as of the fall of 1988 of the number of homeless people in Gainesville and Alachua County, but there was a consensus that this population has grown significantly in the last few years and now far outnumbers the shelter beds available. Recently a sharp increase in homeless families has been observed.

"Gainesville's increase in the number of homeless is probably due to the depressed economic system," says Michele Benefield, executive director, Neighborhood Housing Services of Gainesville, Inc. "There are a lot of people who can't pay rent or mortgage and feed their kids. It's just too expensive. People think the homeless are lazy and don't want to work. That is not true," he added.

The Gainesville Search for Shelter effort is aimed at providing 18 emergency beds—a significant number considering there are only 58 emergency beds in the county when the decision was made. In addition, the project would upgrade a shelter kitchen that provided lunch to 75 to 150 persons a day.

Under study is St. Francis House, a nonprofit shelter located across the street from a major downtown revitalization project. The developer and tenants of that project look unfavorably upon St. Francis House, even though it currently houses only 14 persons. Adding more beds would most likely increase that hostility, so providing an unobtrusive addition is a main priority. But since any sizeable addition will just barely fit on the site, alternative locations are being considered.

St. Francis House plans to continue its lunch service to nonresidents and has requested a commercial kitchen in an effort to increase efficiency. For the first time dining space for up to 50 persons would be available, thus lowering neighbors' discontentment about meal guests wandering onto their private property. Also for the first time, St. Francis House would provide toilet, shower, and storage facilities for those who cannot be sheltered. Social service referrals for both residents and nonresidents would be offered on site. Construction costs are estimated at $250,000.

The task group will continue meeting on a monthly basis until shelter facilities for the homeless match the needs of the Gainesville community.

CONTACT
Fred Vyverberg, AIA
2277 Northwest 16th Avenue
Gainesville, Fla. 32605
(904) 376-8384

SPONSORS & PARTICIPANTS
Alachua County Affordable Housing
  Coalition
Alachua County Housing Authority
Catholic Charities
City of Gainesville
Corner Drugstore
First Union Bank
Florida State Department of Corrections
Gainesville Chapter/AIA
Gainesville Fire Department
Gainesville Home Builders' Association
Mental Health Association
NHS of Gainesville, Inc.
St. Francis House
St. Michael's Church
University of Florida Chapter/AIAS

WEST ELEVATION

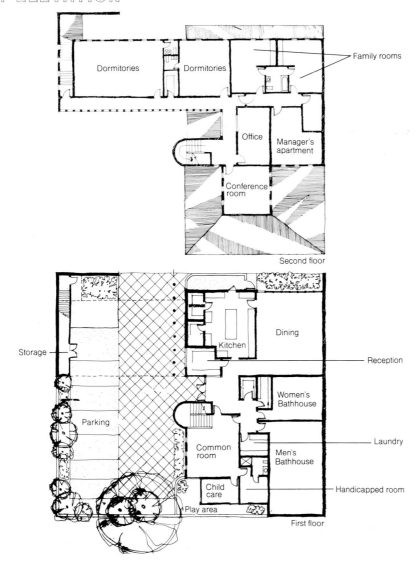

Dormitories

Dormitories

Family rooms

Office

Manager's apartment

Conference room

Second floor

Storage

Parking

Kitchen

Dining

Reception

Women's Bathhouse

Laundry

Common room

Men's Bathhouse

Handicapped room

Child care

Play area

First floor

29

# ATLANTA, GEORGIA

Of the 5,000 to 8,000 homeless persons in Atlanta, 41 percent are thought to be war veterans; yet, there is no housing designed specifically for veterans who want to make the transition from homelessness to being housed. Ideally, such housing would also provide on-site social services for veterans.

The Atlanta Search for Shelter task force joined with Veterans Upward Bound, a nonprofit group that has provided services to veterans for 14 years. The long-term goal was threefold: (1) provide stable housing for homeless veterans for up to 18 months; (2) help each veteran achieve independent living through employment training, other educational courses, personal counseling, and budget management, among other services; and (3) provide follow-up services to each veteran who leaves the shelter.

Two buildings currently occupied by Veterans Upward Bound were chosen for the new shelter—a small three-bedroom house and an old hospital. The house is in need of general cosmetic renovation and some reallocation of interior space. The hospital needs to be renovated thoroughly. For economic reasons the interior partitions of the hospital are to be retained as much as possible.

The guiding principle was to develop a design that "encourages personal autonomy in the midst of an organized program for change and emphasizes a homelike atmosphere rather than an institutional one." Three types of housing are to be provided: a group house (for six persons), private sleeping rooms (for 13 or 14), and a dormitory (for six).

The Georgia Institute of Technology team turned the small house into a group home for six veterans with three bedrooms, a living room, kitchen, and dining room. The hospital would then house the remaining 19 to 20 veterans in single rooms and a dorm and would have dining facilities, a kitchen, bathroom, reception area, and four classrooms. Facades would blend with the commercial strip on Martin Luther King Drive (the south end of the property) and the residences on Harwell Street (the north end of the property). The building is zoned commercial and will be renovated to meet building codes that apply to hotels.

Rehabilitation is expected to cost $230,000. Funding will include an $86,250 grant from the U.S. Department of Housing and Urban Development Transitional Housing Demonstration Program, a $71,875 grant from the city of Atlanta from its share of the federal community development block grant program, and a low-interest loan for $71,875 from the Georgia Residential Finance Authority's Revolving Loan to Assist the Homeless.

Operation costs will be covered by a $23,202 grant each year for five years from HUD's Transitional Housing Demonstration Program; $5,700 per year from the National Scholarship Service/Fund for Negro Students, Inc.; $13,000 per year from Transition House, Inc., a project of the Atlanta Episcopal Diocese and the Atlanta Presbytery and operator of the shelter with Veterans Upward Bound; and the $25,000 of rent expected from residents per year, much of which will come from social services benefits for veterans.

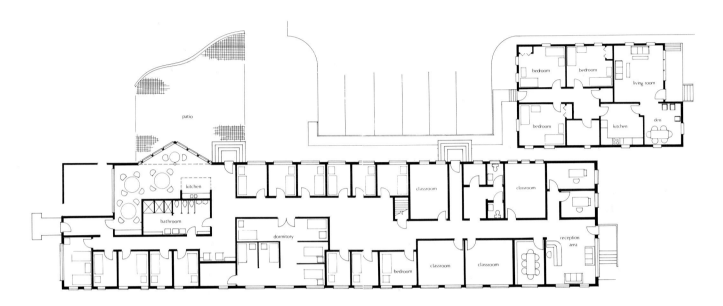

*This shelter for veterans would consist of a renovated three-bedroom house, upper right, and hospital, larger building above.*

CONTACT
Richard Bradfield, AIA
Bradfield Associates, Inc.
P.O. Box 52426
Atlanta, Ga. 30355
(404) 231-5202

SPONSORS & PARTICIPANTS
Atlanta Chapter/AIA
Atlanta Task Force for the Homeless:
    Dr. Jim Beatty
Bradfield Associates: Richard Bradfield,
    AIA, Shad Funkhouser, Greg
    Richards
Chung, Cheng, Chang, Architects: Sandy
    Shobe
Cooper Carry & Associates, Inc.: Sharon
J. Ferguson, Walter B. Jones Jr., Bobbie Unger
Deckbar/McCormack, Inc.: Gerard T.
    Deckbar
Georgia Institute of Technology,
    AIAS/Chapter
Georgia Institute of Technology, College
    of Architecture. Faculty: Rufus R.
    Hughes, AIA
Osborn Associates, Inc.: Samuel E.
    Osborn, AIA
SRO Housing, Inc.: Steve Cleghorn
Stevens & Wilkinson, Inc.: Jack W.
    Smith, AIA
Veterans Upward Bound
John Ware & Associates, Inc.: Gita N.
    Hendessi

# CHICAGO, ILLINOIS

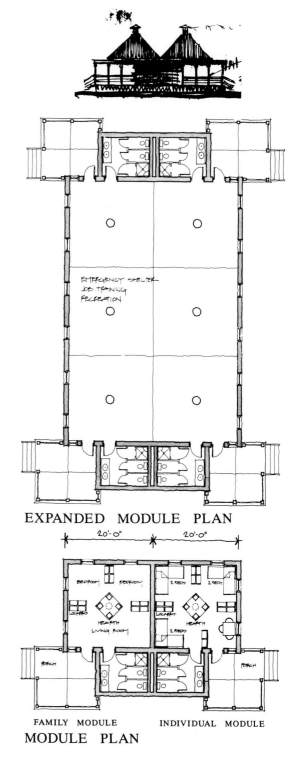

**EXPANDED MODULE PLAN**

**FAMILY MODULE** · **INDIVIDUAL MODULE**

**MODULE PLAN**

Like most major U.S. cities, Chicago has among its population large numbers and various types of homeless persons—from 12,000 to 25,000. Thus, the Chicago Search for Shelter task force decided to address several types of shelters for the homeless: emergency shelters, transitional shelters, and single-room-occupancy dwellings. Joining in the effort were local architects, service providers, government officials, and architecture students and educators from Chicago, St. Louis, Milwaukee, and Cincinnati.

Each type of shelter had certain design requirements, which reflected many of the universally acknowledged needs for each type of shelter.

*Emergency Shelter.* A shelter type that provides temporary, overnight accommodation and operates between 7:00 pm to 7:00 am. Essential requirements include the following:
• dormitory style, with cots in an open room or in a large room with partitions to accommodate large numbers of homeless persons
• separate zones for men and women
• capability for shelters to be used for other purposes when demand is low
• sleeping areas for 100 beds with a minimum of 50 square feet per bed
• adequate toilet and shower facilities
• lockers for personal storage
• private counseling rooms
• sufficiently sized entry areas for the guests
• a high-capacity laundry room
• area for clothing and food distribution
• kitchen and dining areas
• private staff rooms
• medical examination room
• daytime drop-in center.

*Above, simple modules can be arranged to accommodate emergency and transitional housing. Right, a rowhouse-turned-transitional shelter with a centrally located court.*

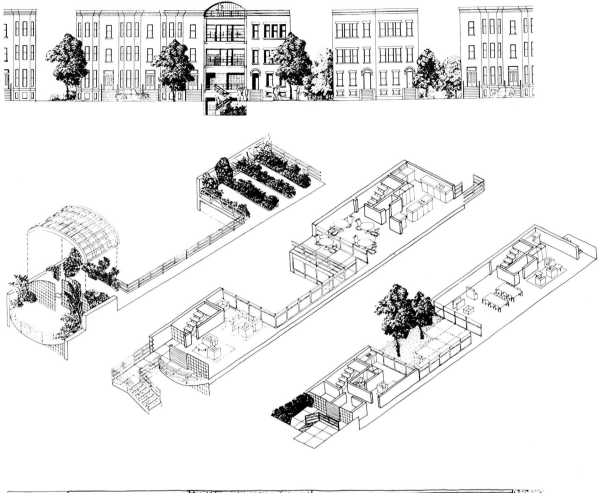

COMMUNITY LEVEL

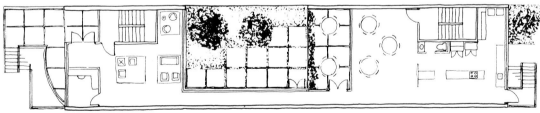

*Transitional Shelter for Families.* A shelter type comparable to the settlement houses for indigent families in the early part of the century. Essential requirements include the following:
• neighborhood setting (preferable)
• separate sleeping rooms for family members, grouped in clusters (suites) or accessible to a living space common to several families
• security
• maximum stay 120 days

• maximum capacity 65 beds
• shared bathrooms
• communal kitchens
• dining areas
• office and counseling rooms
• entry area for the guests
• indoor day-care facility, with the minimum of 35 square feet per child
• outdoor play and recreation areas
• meeting rooms for group discussions, adult education, training, and counseling.

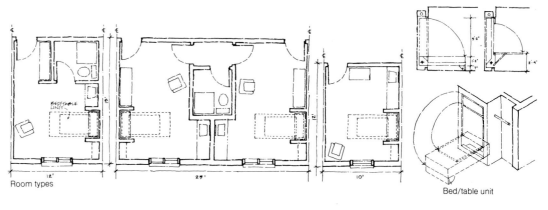

Room types

Bed/table unit

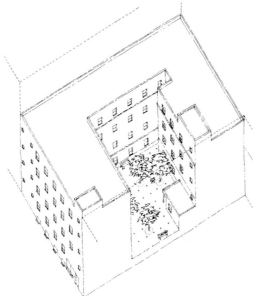

Single-room-occupancy residence

*Single-Room-Occupancy Residences.* In the past this housing type was often described as transient hotels, flop houses, or men's hotels. Many were actually modest apartment hotels, and some were even considered elegant. Traditionally, these hotels have housed immigrants, migrant workers, fixed-income individuals, and single people. The proposed SRO is to serve the population currently housed in two hotels that contain more than 100 rooms but that are located in the downtown section where the new main branch of the city's public library will be located. Essential requirements for the new building include the following:

• 100 single rooms
• individual or shared bathrooms
• individual food storage and communal food preparation areas
• individual storage facilities
• private offices for staff
• front desk with mail and message services
• rooms for group activities
• laundry room
• outdoor recreation and sitting areas
• a community lounge and other spaces that create a sense of community.

34

East elevation

Second/third floor plan

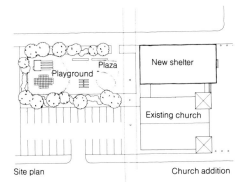

Site plan                    Church addition

CONTACT
John Tomassi, AIA
Chicago Architectural Assistance Center
410 S. Michigan Ave.
Chicago, Ill. 60605
(312) 786-1920

SPONSORS & PARTICIPANTS
Chicago Architectural Assistance Center
Chicago Chapter/AIA
Chicago Planning Department
Louis Gutierez, Alderman, 25th Ward
Gerald Horn, FAIA
Illinois Institute of Technology, School
    of Architecture, Planning, and Design
Illinois Institute of Technology
    Chapter/AIAS
Metropolitan Planning Council
Walter Netsch, FAIA
St. Martin DePorres House
Unity Shelter
University of Illinois-Chicago, School
    of Architecture
University of Illinois-Chicago Chapter/
    AIAS
University of Wisconsin, Milwaukee,
    School of Architecture and Urban
    Planning

In the hills and valleys of Appalachia a large percentage of the population lives in substandard housing — buildings with no indoor plumbing, inefficient heating, faulty chimneys, leaking roofs, defective water systems, and major structural deficiencies. In addition many houses are on flood plains, in slip-prone areas, beneath loose rock formations, and in close proximity to combustible forest materials. Taking an active interest in righting these wrongs is the Lexington Search for Shelter team, consisting of members of the College of Architecture (ARCH), University of Kentucky, and Appalachia — Science in the Public Interest (ASPI), an environmental center in Livingston, Ky.

ASPI assists the Sand Hill Community Land Trust in the design and construction of low-cost housing for people of modest income. The trust owns 150 acres in central Appalachia in the Daniel Boone National Forest and on the Rockcastle River. The river is popular with canoers and fishermen; part of it has been designated by the state as a "wild and scenic river." Many people in the community are of Cherokee Indian ancestry. Part of the land trust contains graves of Cherokee ancestors and is considered sacred by the tribe.

Livingston, the nearest town, is the only one in Kentucky with no inhabitants above the poverty level. At the same time both of the surrounding counties — Laurel and Rockcastle — have a severely limited supply of low-cost housing.

While the focus of the effort by ARCH and ASPI is low-income housing for single families, there is also a concern for the overall enhancement of each community. Therefore, ARCH and

ASPI provide comprehensive community assessments and designs—proper housing siting, gardens and orchards, park and recreation space, access roads, and a community center.

The location of the Lexington Search for Shelter effort is a rocky, steep area depopulated by a wave of migration, a devastating tornado in 1974, and the loss of fertility of the steep-sloped farmland. It is currently an underpopulated area.

Those with immediate housing needs—those who live in dilapidated houses or who have limited space for a growing family—are chosen to participate in the Rockcastle Valley project. Each applicant must follow strict rules: Keep the house clean and free of litter, make monthly payments, and abide in an environmentally responsible manner of treating the land and its coal resources carefully.

The following seven principles are to guide housing design:
• simplicity in construction principles to allow for replication by other home owners and for owner involvement in construction;
• low-cost construction;
• use of native materials to diminish costs and allow for easy replication;
• access to major highways for increased employment opportunities and reduction of isolation;
• resistance to fire;
• resistance to theft;
• energy consciousness.

The on-site analysis focused on determining what indigenous materials were available for construction. Wood, rock, and clay exist in great abundance. Since wood is easily combustible, it was re-

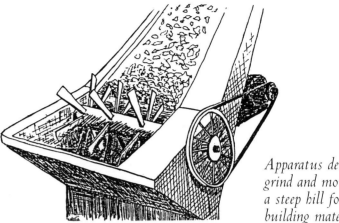

*Apparatus developed to grind and move clay up a steep hill for use as a building material.*

jected as a major building material. The noncombustible character of clay was favored, and several clay beds exist on the site. Moreover, great savings can be realized by using available materials for construction.

In the end, the team concluded that a site analysis does lead to more appropriate solutions in low-cost housing in rural settings; one advantage is the readily available supply of land and resources. The Search for Shelter team plans to see the project through the design and construction phases.

CONTACT
Jim Burris, AIA
Burris Associates
1017C Trotwood Drive
Lexington, Ky. 40511
(606) 231-0323

SPONSORS & PARTICIPANTS
Appalachia—Science in the Public Interest (ASPI)
University of Kentucky, College of Architecture (ARCH). Students: Sara Coppler, Iain Dickie, Bernie Engelman, Lambert Graham, Craig Thomas, Paul Woodrum. Faculty: Anthony Roccanova
University of Kentucky Chapter/AIAS

# NEW ORLEANS, LOUISIANA

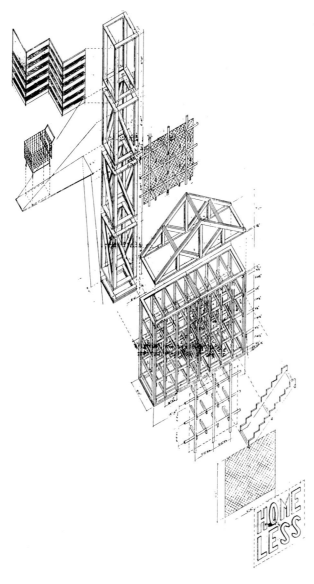

The New Orleans Search for Shelter workshop was perhaps more theoretical than practical but nonetheless contributes to the ongoing dialogue concerning appropriate ways to house the homeless.

"The homeless in New Orleans deserve a network," one team suggested. "Not a network of dumpsters and soup kitchens, but a network of mobile units reaching out to the missions, the overpass, the abandoned homes—a fleet of straight-body trucks, modified to the hilt." These trucks would be equipped with showers, a library, a kitchen, and counseling and medical facilities. At the end of the day, the fleet would pull into an empty warehouse and be used as individual sleeping quarters.

"How can we fight homelessness by providing substandard shelters that still leave the homeless on the streets?" a second team asked. "Are we addressing the problem or just perpetuating it? Is it an architectural or a societal issue?" To provoke a public response to the debate, the team proposed placing a billboard in a highly visible location. This three-dimensional billboard would feature a compressed wood framework of a house, inside of which would be mattresses resting on rafters. Leading to the house would be treadless stairs symbolizing the hopelessness and despair connected to homelessness. A sense of hopefulness would also be suggested—a feeling that homelessness can begin to be solved if society makes an effort to provide treads for the stairs. Other symbolic elements on the billboard would be a shopping cart, a tower draped with an abstract American flag, and a digital display sign that provides daily infor-

*Above, three-dimensional billboard designed to draw attention to the plight of the homeless. Right, two designs for city sleepers: At night one lifts the sleeping area up a pole; the other swivels open.*

mation about the homeless in New Orleans.

Another team studied an existing shelter consisting of six shotgun cottages and recommended the addition of a common kitchen and dining space in the center unit and a clearer outdoor circulation plan. The last team designed a city sleeper modeled after a concept put forth by San Francisco architect Donald MacDonald, FAIA—a simple enclosure in which a homeless person can sleep by night and which is easily transportable by day.

CONTACT
Michael Crosby
Tulane University
School of Architecture
New Orleans, La. 70118
(504) 865-5389

SPONSORS & PARTICIPANTS
Tulane University Chapter/AIAS
Tulane University, School of Archi-
    tecture

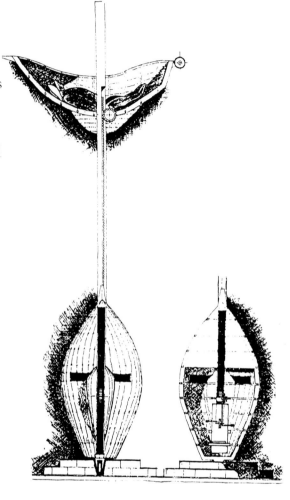

# SHREVEPORT, LOUISIANA

The Shreveport Search for Shelter workshop has had far-reaching results: the first public recognition by the mayor that a large number of homeless people roam the city streets, a broader public acknowledgment that solutions need to be found soon, and a commitment from one of the city's leading developers to begin that process by transforming a dilapidated hotel into long-term housing in the form of single-room-occupancy units.

Shreveport's participation in the Search for Shelter was actually first advocated by that developer, Mary Nesbitt, who wanted to save the historically significant McAdoo Hotel. Nesbitt was well aware of the increasing demand for low-income housing in Shreveport at a time when little was being done to increase the affordable housing supply. She was so eager to learn whether the McAdoo project could work financially and programmatically that the Shreveport Search for Shelter workshop was held months before the others (and, therefore, is considered the program's pilot project).

Over the last few years Shreveport's economy has suffered, in large part because of the drop in oil prices and the slowdown of oil production. This economic downturn is quite visible in the downtown core—where many of the older, low-rise storefronts are boarded up, where few new skyscrapers are present on the skyline, and where a new, upscale, and once potentially profitable, shopping district has struggled to survive.

An even clearer indication of the economic depression is the city's housing situation. Many of the elegant houses of the once prosperous are now for sale. And despite strong renovation efforts of local nonprofit and government housing groups (most notably, the renovation of shotgun houses in the historic Ledbetter Heights area), a large portion of the city's poor live in substandard housing.

These conditions have resulted in a growing number of homeless and inadequately housed people—single men and women, battered women and children, the chronically mentally ill, the elderly. Yet the city made no official assessment of the housing situation—made no attempt to discover who these people are, what their housing needs might be, and how these needs could be met. It was the Search for Shelter project that sparked the beginning of such an investigation.

At the Search for Shelter workshop's public forum in July 1987, Mayor John Hussey admitted that he had previously been unaware of the city's homeless problem. Prompted by the workshop, the mayor called for the city's first survey of the homeless, which estimated that at any given time there are 1,000 homeless persons.

Other speakers such as Sister Margaret McCaffrey of the city's Christian Services suggested that the number vulnerable to homelessness is significantly higher. "More than 1,600 families are desperate for homes," she said, admonishing the city for not having group housing for the chronically mentally ill or enough shelters for battered women. "Each person has a right to a home, to experience his or her own dignity," she said.

At the time the waiting list of appli-

**Austin Street Elevation**

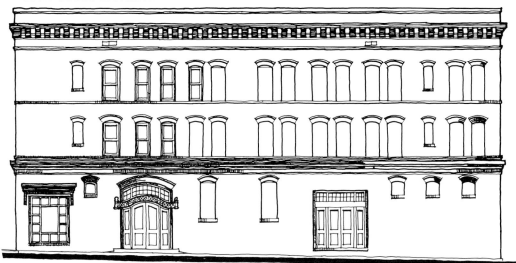

cants seeking public housing bore 800 names; the vacancy rate for the city housing authority's 775 public units hovered around 5 percent.

During that public forum it quickly became clear that the McAdoo Hotel project could improve the living conditions of only a small portion of the city's homeless. At the same time, however, the Search for Shelter project began to symbolize a new approach to eradicating substandard living conditions, one that relies on contributions from the public, private, and nonprofit sectors.

Sam Galbreath, director of housing for the Portland (Ore.) Development Commission, said the workshop "fostered community awareness, built coalitions among its movers and shakers, and inspired completion of the project to the point that the community won't be able to say no."

The McAdoo Hotel is an 18,200-square-foot, three-story, 1920s brick building that is structurally sound but extremely dilapidated and currently

vacant. It is located on Texas Avenue, a main but ailing artery connecting several outlying neighborhoods with the central business district. The hotel also stands on the edge of Ledbetter Heights, a neighborhood containing historically significant shotgun houses, many of which have been renovated for low-income housing under the auspices of a nonprofit development group.

The McAdoo Hotel also shares a street with the Oakland/Austin Streets Historic Preservation district, a collection of beautifully restored Victorian houses, now containing small businesses. At the public forum the district president opposed the renovation of the McAdoo as an SRO hotel, arguing that such a development would hurt the financial viability of the historic district.

At the time of the workshop the specific population for the McAdoo was undetermined, so workshop participants addressed the needs of several types of residents—the chronically mentally ill, the elderly, single men, families, battered

41

Telephones
Elevator

Second floor

Service entrance                    Alley

Telephones

Shop

Manager's
apartments

Kitchen

Social service
offices

Office

Library                                         Lobby

Elevator

Grocery

First floor

women, and children. Each team was asked to consider the following concerns:
• the need to design dignified housing;
• the relationship of the McAdoo to its surrounding environment;
• the need to preserve the historic character of the McAdoo in order to qualify for historic preservation tax credits;
• the need to mitigate the adverse impact of a greater number of cars in the area—cars of tenants and employees.

Basically, the six teams suggested that most of the room partitions on the upper two floors (the residential floors) remain the same, with some alterations to allow for common lounge areas. Since the McAdoo was originally a residential hotel, the current layout of the second and third floors appears to be well suited for reuse; by keeping floor plan changes to a minimum, construction costs would be reduced. Currently the second and third floors each have 21 bedrooms and eight baths (three are private and five are shared). A few bedrooms would be lost on each floor to make space for the lounges. The rooms have high ceilings and large windows, which provide more than adequate natural ventilation and light.

The first floor could easily be broken into zones to provide a secure entrance to the hotel and space for one or two commercial enterprises. The rent paid by those commercial enterprises would help lower the tenants' rent.

The most challenging design problem was what to do with the first floor's skylit atrium space, the roof of which forms an outdoor courtyard for the second floor. One group opened the atrium all the way to the third floor; another created an outdoor, protected deck on the second floor for use by the residents or as a day-care playground.

To increase their sensitivity, workshop participants visited the Creswell Hotel, a nearby SRO hotel, and the Hospitality House, the area's soup kitchen. The Louisiana Tech architecture students who participated in the workshop stayed at the Creswell.

The design teams' work was so well received that developer Nesbitt, previously interested but unsure about the viability of renovating the McAdoo as an SRO, announced her commitment to the project at the workshop's end. She acted on her option to buy the hotel, and many of the Search for Shelter workshop's suggestions were incorporated into the final design scheme. Renovation costs were estimated at $600,000. Construction began in February 1988.

CONTACT
Kim Mitchell, AIA
Morgan, O'Neal, Hill & Sutton
1010 CNB Building
Shreveport, La. 71101
(318) 221-1623

SPONSORS & PARTICIPANTS
Christian Services: Sister Margaret McCaffrey
City of Shreveport: Mayor John Hussey
Fairfield Property Management: Kathy Poss
George Jackson Architects: Ken Irvin
Landmark Rehabilitation Project, Inc.
Louisiana Institute of Technology, School of Architecture. Faculty: Robert Fakelmann, Robert Moran, Peter Schneider

Louisiana Institute of Technology Chapter/AIAS
Morgan, O'Neal, Hill & Sutton Architects: Kim E. Mitchell
NHS of Shreveport, Inc.
The Newman Partnership: Lauren F. Marchive, III
Nesbitt Management Co.: Melissa Flournoy, Mary Nesbitt
Schuldt Associates: Art Schuldt Jr.
Shreveport Chapter/AIA
Shreveport Housing Authority
Shreveport Jaycees
Shreveport Neighborhood Housing Services: David Lewis
SRO Housing Los Angeles: Andy Raubeson
SRO Housing Portland, Ore.: Sam Galbreath

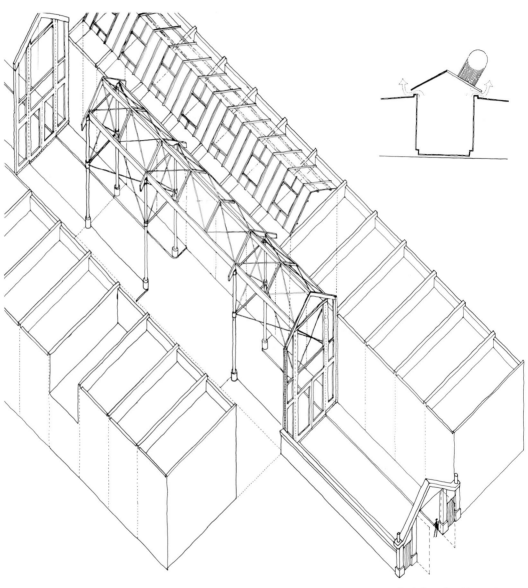

Booth Street Row Houses

The need for housing for the homeless is so great in Baltimore that the city's Neighborhood Progress Administration is considering transforming a block of abandoned row houses into affordable housing. This project and three others scattered around the city were the focus of the Baltimore Search for Shelter workshop. The teams consisted of architecture students and faculty from the University of Maryland and Morgan State University and area architects and service providers.

*Booth Street Row Houses.* This hypothetical project called for abandoned sections of alley-block row houses to be renovated for emergency shelter for families and individuals in dormitories and SRO units. The block in question is approximately 11,500 square feet. Costs are estimated at $517,500. The program called for the north and south rows to be linked by a common skylit roof to create an all-weather community room.

*Antioch Church Shelter and Home.* Located in a large house adjacent to a park and playground, this 10,000-square-foot shelter houses 65 persons. It is one of only three shelters in the Baltimore area that accepts households headed by men. Current inadequacies include the lack of dining and public spaces, a small area for staff, and sufficient storage space. The estimated cost of renovation is $650,000. One of the designs called for moveable units, like big closets, that would become walls dividing living and sleeping spaces and that could be used for storage.

*Portions of two parallel rowhouses would be joined by a skylight. The space beneath would be a community room.*

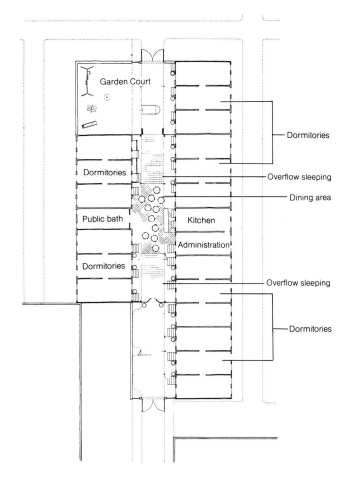

45

*Church of the Guardian Angel.* This transitional shelter for families houses about 25 persons in a 9,500-square-foot area. The objective here was to encourage a sense of stability and privacy for the families by distinguishing private, semiprivate, and semipublic zones in a graded manner within the facility. Renovation costs are estimated at $20 per square foot or $150,000.

*Rutland Elementary School.* When renovated, the 83,141-square-foot school is to house 119 family members. The average length of stay will be six months.

The overall aim is to approximate, as nearly as possible, traditional living quarters and to encourage economic and emotional self-sufficiency. Resources available to the families include counseling, day care, and employment training programs. Renovation costs were estimated at $3,325,640, or approximately $40 per square foot.

Further refinement of the workshop results may lead to construction if the city government provides money for the project from the $1 million in federal grants it received for city programs.

CONTACT
Ann Von Lossberg
Neighborhood Design Center
416 East 31st Street
Baltimore, Md. 21218
(301) 366-3223

SPONSORS & PARTICIPANTS
Action for the Homeless: Kevin Woodward
Baltimore Chapter/AIA
Baltimore Jobs in Energy Project: Chris Smith
Bignell & Watkins Architects: Michael Bignell, Adeniyi Paul, Ravi Waldon
Cochran Stephenson & Donkervoet, Inc.
Catholic University Chapter/AIAS
Gould Architects: Beth Glasser
LaPicki/Smith Associates: Don Smith
May & Holbrook Architects
Morgan State University. Faculty: Gil Cooke, Anthony Johns
Morgan State University Chapter/AIAS
Neighborhood Progress Administration, City of Baltimore
Neighborhood Design Center: Jacek Ghosh
Neighborhood Housing Services of Baltimore: Michael Braswell
Neighborhood Progress Administration
RTKL Associates, Inc.: Gary Bowden, Chuck Butler, Tim Rommel
Schamu, Machowski & Doo Associates: Victor Greco, Kirk Irwin
Sulton Campbell & Associates: Charles Owens
University of Maryland, School of Architecture. Faculty: Fred Johns
University of Maryland Chapter/AIAS

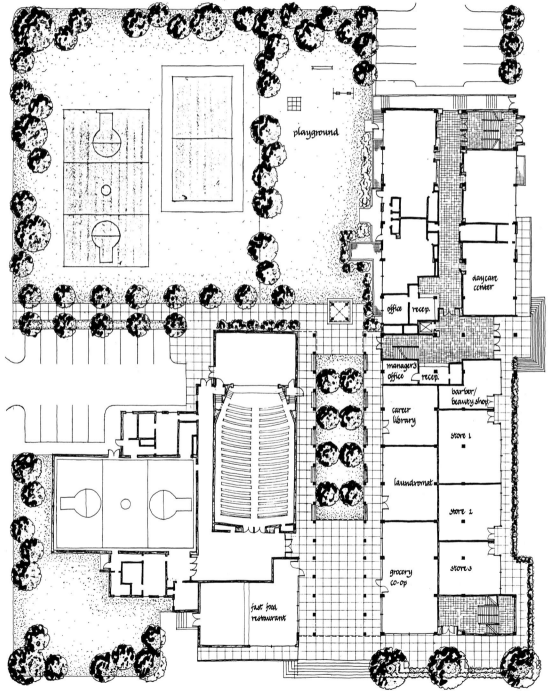

playground

daycare
center

office   recep.

manager's
office   recep.

barber/
beauty shop

career
library

store 1

laundromat

store 2

grocery
co-op

store 3

fast food
restaurant

Rutland Elementary School

# BOSTON, MASSACHUSETTS

In Boston the Search for Shelter workshop sponsored a design competition for architecture students from the Boston Architectural Center, Harvard Graduate School of Design, and Wentworth Institute of Technology. The subject was transitional shelter for approximately 15 families, each of which has a single female adult and small children.

Basic design requirements included a facility for on-site training in business skills, personal management, financial skills, parenting, and health care services. Suggested common areas include a large living room, a small kitchen, a children's playroom and limited on-site day care, a library, a "quiet" area, a laundry room, and an outdoor play area for children.

A unique characteristic of the shelter is that ultimately it will become permanent housing, owned and managed by the residents. At that point some of the space allotted to supportive services would become commercial with rental income helping pay co-op expenses.

Workshop participants were asked to incorporate in their designs the following requirements:
• develop areas of community focus—i.e., spaces that enhance community spirit;
• accommodate the privacy needs of individuals within the family and of families within the larger community;
• acknowledge the need for spaces that can be personalized;
• help establish a sense of pride in one's home;
• consider how support areas can evolve into commercial spaces;
• ease the relationship between residents and the community;
• provide space that is conducive to socialization for children of different ages (more than 40 children living there);
• use spatial flow to enhance (but not intrude on) social interaction.

M.I.T. School of Architecture

48

CONTACT
Wendell Phillips, AIA
Wendell Phillips & Associates, Inc.
2 Central Square
Cambridge, Mass. 02139
(617) 576-3210

SPONSORS & PARTICIPANTS
Boston Architectural Center
Boston Architectural Center Chapter/
AIAS
Boston Housing Authority
Boston Society of Architects
CBT Associates: Doug Fisher
City of Boston, Emergency Shelter
Commission
City of Boston, Executive Office of Com-
munities and Development
Emergency Shelter Commission: Susan
Tracy
Harvard University, Graduate School
of Design
Hichox Williams Architects: Brigid
Williams

Housing Allowance Project
Richard Leaf, AIA
Massachusetts Institute of Technology,
School of Architecture
Massachusetts Institute of Technology
Chapter/AIAS
Massachusetts State Association of
Architects
Neighborhood Housing Services
Susan Oleksiw
Payette Associates: John Wilson, AIA
R. Wendell Phillips & Associates: R.
Wendell Phillips
Pine Street Inn: Rand Baily
The Sullivan Trust: Valery Dionne-
Lanier
Wentworth Institute of Technology.
Faculty: George Balich, AIA, L. Lane
Grover, Herbert Kronish, AIA
Wentworth Institute of Technology
Chapter/AIAS
Women's Institute for Housing and Eco-
nomic Development: Joan Forrester
Sprague

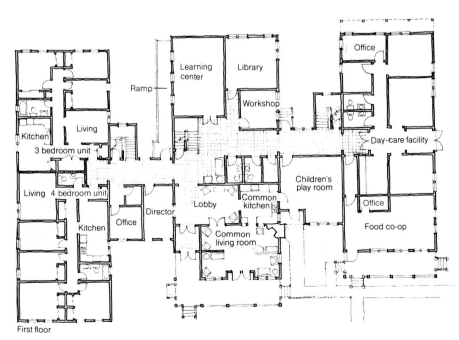

First floor

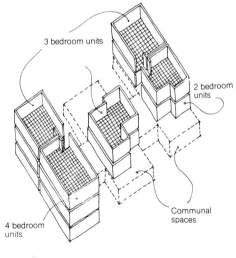

3 bedroom units

2 bedroom units

4 bedroom units

Communal spaces

*Transitional housing for families in three bungalows, across page, is connected on first floor, left. Above, bedroom types.*

49

# PONTIAC, MICHIGAN

In Pontiac and surrounding Oakland County, transitional housing for the homeless is practically nonexistent. Therefore, the Pontiac Search for Shelter task group choose as its project the renovation of a former apartment building into a transitional shelter to be known as Pontiac Area Transitional Housing (PATH).

The brick apartment building on Cottage Street currently has a mix of small apartments and efficiencies. It is in a state of disrepair and is presently condemned.

The workshop focused on:
• providing a flexible, secure environment for homeless people for three to six months;
• encouraging personal development, leading to placement in long-term housing and the ability to earn a regular income;
• fostering independence through social interaction and the development of job and living skills; and
• providing a realistic solution that is economic and flexible.

In an effort to explore several design possibilities, the workshop participants were divided into four groups, each concentrating on different design concepts.

Group A was asked to develop dormitory accommodations, two administrative offices, and a reception area, with space for a nurses' station and a day-care facility in an adjacent home. Unique characteristics are a side entry with access to the day care area and a greenhouse within the existing staircase.

Group B was to develop suites for a single mother and her children and individual rooms for single adults. An administrative cubicle and a conference room were required; social services, including a job placement facility, would exist in the neighborhood.

Group C examined efficiencies that could be converted into two-bedroom suites. To be included were administrative offices and a conference room, a private meeting space that could be used by a visiting nurse, and a day-care facility.

Group D was asked to accommodate several population types in single units and suites. The design would encompass a resident manager with living facilities and three administrative offices. The house adjacent to the apartment building would be a day care center. Family counseling would be offered nearby.

The Pontiac Search for Shelter task force plans to see the project through to completion. PATH will continue to be studied by students at the Lawrence Institute of Technology. Early estimates of renovation costs range from $250,000 to $300,000. The facility is currently owned by the nonprofit organization Lighthouse, which will manage the building after its renovation.

The project has received the support of Pontiac's mayor, the Oakland County Mental Health Department, Michigan Department of Social Services, and St. Joseph Mercy Hospital Center. Mayor Walter Moore in a declaration praised the Pontiac Search for Shelter task group for its "collaborative effort in providing secure, welcome housing to help restore the pride and dignity of homeless people and assist them in their return to independent living." Funding will be sought from HUD, the Michigan State Housing Development Authority, and private foundations.

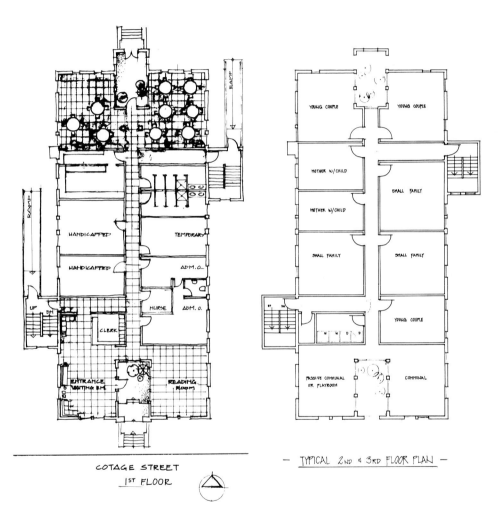

COTAGE STREET
1ST FLOOR

— TYPICAL 2ND & 3RD FLOOR PLAN —

CONTACT
John Dziurman, AIA
Wade-Trim/Dzuirman
155 Romeo Road
Rochester, Mich. 48063
(313) 652-8777

SPONSORS & PARTICIPANTS
Capuchin Community Soup Kitchen
Citizens Coalition Federal Credit Union
City of Pontiac
City of Lighthouse
Coalition of Temporary Shelter
Detroit Chapter/AIA

Pamela Y. Dubois, AIA
Lawrence Institute of Technology, School
    of Architecture. Faculty: Karl
    Greimel, FAIA, Betty-Lee Sydler-
    Sweatt, AIA. Student: Paul Matelic
Lawrence Institute of Technology
    Chapter/AIAS
Oakland County Department of Social
    Services
National Coalition for the Homeless:
    Lewis Hickson
Neighborhood Reinvestment: Saundra
    A. Willingham
Wade-Trim/Dzuirman: John Dziurman

51

# MINNEAPOLIS—ST. PAUL, MINNESOTA

In the twin cities, five Search for Shelter teams examined the renovation of five buildings into emergency and transitional shelters.

*Mary Hall.* An L-shaped, five-story, brick building, Mary Hall was once used as a dormitory for nurses training at a nearby hospital. It is currently used as an emergency shelter for men; Catholic Charities, however, would like to provide shelter for women and families, too. Most important in a renovation scheme was the separation of the men from the women and children.

The Search for Shelter team called for the realignment of interior spaces with a locked door separating the men from the women and children. Some dormitory space had to be removed to provide more kitchen, storage, laundry, and community spaces.

*2421 Portland South Street, Minneapolis.* A typical apartment building would be transformed into transitional housing for mothers and children. At the center of the building is a two-story community room with a domestic hearth. Additional warmth would be provided by natural light emitted through the large southern-facing windows. The elimination of the double-loaded corridor and the combining of separate living and dining rooms into one space created additional sleeping rooms.

*The Salvation Army Lodge.* This building in St. Paul is to be renovated into a crisis and transitional shelter for women and children. "Given the limits of the budget and an increased need for support services, we set up an analogy to one's own house, looking at the individual beds as rooms in a house and considering the lodge as a neighborhood," the Search for Shelter team said. In this scheme the hallways become "streets" and each room a "house." The door to each room is given a "porch" treatment, making it unique from the rest. The treatment is carried into the room with texture and color. The guests are encouraged to decorate their bedspace "room" with personal items.

"The dignity of the residents is established by having control over their environment," the team continues. "They are free to move anywhere within the facility, just as one is free to roam through their neighborhood, respecting, of course, one's neighbors. A sense of security is maintained by a single point of entry."

*Theresa Living Center.* This transitional shelter for women with young children is housed in a former convent. Its 15 rooms and the community spaces were determined to be adequate for the shelter. Outside protected space, however, was missing. Therefore the design calls for an enclosed courtyard surrounded by dense vegetation.

*St. Anne Convent.* No specific program had been determined for this building, so the Search for Shelter team made a "cookbook" of how different requirements would affect the use of the interior spaces. The team first compared emergency and transitional shelters; both would need a kitchen addition, and the transitional shelter would need a community room addition. "All schemes developed into cruciform plans with the control or orientation point at the center," the team said. This places the hub of activity in the center, a plan that corresponds to the location of a kitchen in a traditional household.

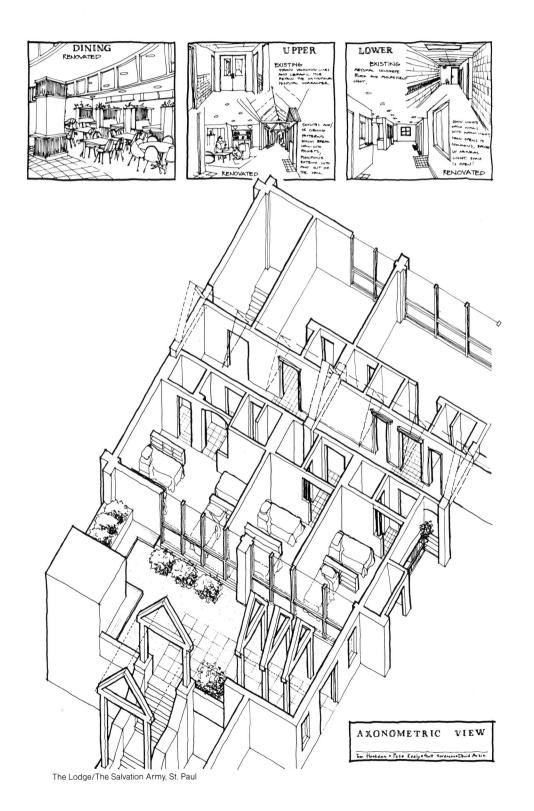

DINING
RENOVATED

UPPER
EXISTING
STRONG VANISHING LINES
AND CERAMIC TILE
RETAIN THE INSTITUTIONAL
HOSPITAL CHARACTER.

SKYLITES AND/
OR CEILING
PATTERNS
WHICH BREAK
HALL INTO
POCKETS.
FUNCTIONS
EXTEND INTO
AND OUT OF
THE HALL.

RENOVATED

LOWER
EXISTING
ABYSMAL CONCRETE
BLOCK AND FLOURESCENT
LIGHT.

DOWN LIGHTS
WASH WALLS
WITH WARM LIGHT
HALL OPENS TO
COMMONS, BRINGS
IN NATURAL
LIGHT, STAIR
IS OPEN.

RENOVATED

AXONOMETRIC VIEW

Tom Hoskens • Pete Keely • Scott Sorenson • David Arkin

The Lodge/The Salvation Army, St. Paul

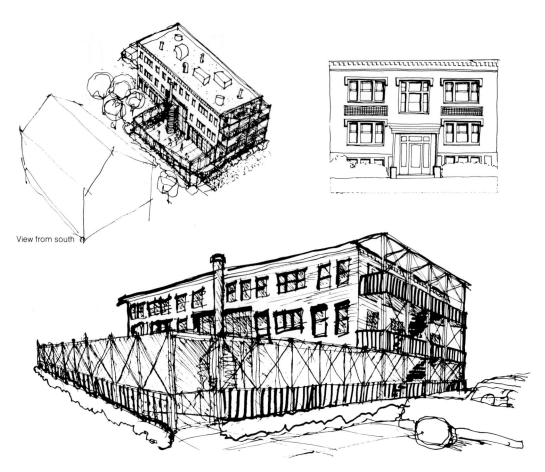

View from south

CONTACT
Louis R. Lundgren, FAIA
The Lundgren Associates Inc.
343 East Kellogg Blvd.
St. Paul, Minn. 55101
(612) 224-4765

SPONSORS & PARTICIPANTS
Michael Anderson, Congressman Vento's
    Office
Anderson Group Architects: Thomas
    Hoskens, AIA
Arvid Ellness Architects: Paul Madsen,
    AIA Catholic Charities: John Spieker
John Cunningham, AIA
Ellerbe, Inc.: Jerry Johnson, AIA
Matt Gilbertson
Grans & Associates: Sally Grans
Dennis Grebner
Kodet Architectural Group: John
    Klockeman, AIA
Lundgren Associates: Cherry Gen
    Lundgren, Louis R. Lundgren, FAIA
Julie Maple
Melander & Melander Architects: David
    A. Schilling, AIA
Metro Council: Neal Cuthbert, Planner
Miller Hansen Westerbeck Architects:
    Larry Westerbeck, AIA

Minneapolis Chapter/AIA
Minneapolis Coalition for the Homeless:
    Mary Jo Jackson
Minneapolis Community Development
    Agency: Kaymarie Colaizy
Neighborhood Housing Service: Bob
    Lee
Northeast Minnesota Chapter/AIA
St. Paul Chapter/AIA
Salvation Army Emergency Lodge: Jan
    Bloom
Team One Members: Tim Bjella, Peter
    Grover, Link Wilson, AIA
Team Two Members: Hadar Karni, Tom
    Peterson, Chris Winter
Team Three Members: Matt Gilbertson,
    Julie Maple, Ken Potts
Team Four Members: David Arkin, Pete
    Keely, Scott Sourenson
Team Five Members: Michael Dant,
    Dian Keehan, Tsi Line Yap
Theresa Living Center: Sister Rita Jirik
Twin Cities NHS, Inc.
University of Minnesota Chapter/AIAS
University of Minnesota, School of
    Architecture and Landscape Arch-
    itecture: David Arkin, Dennis
    Grebner, AIA, Julia Robinson

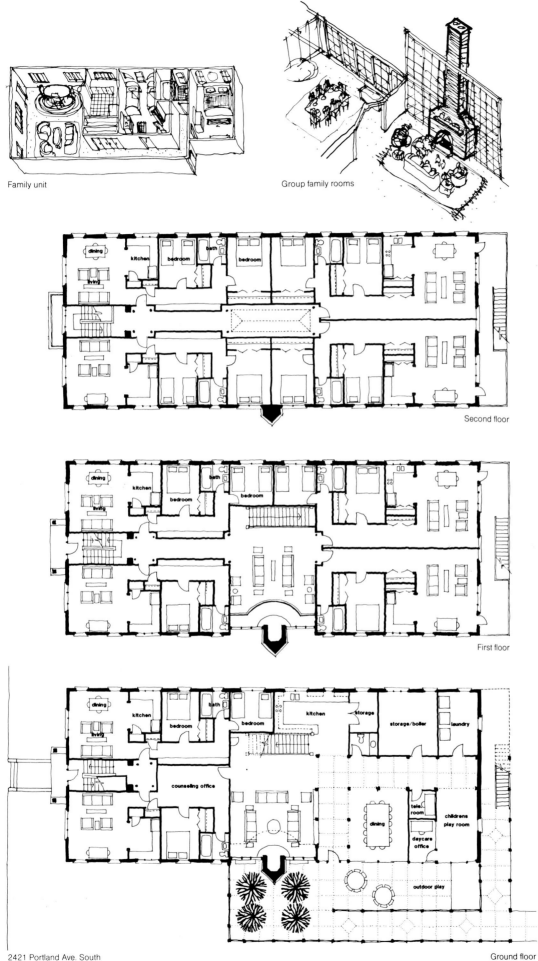

Family unit

Group family rooms

**Second floor**

dining
kitchen
bedroom
bath
bedroom
living

**First floor**

dining
kitchen
bedroom
bath
bedroom
living

**Ground floor**

dining
kitchen
bedroom
bath
bedroom
kitchen
storage
storage/boiler
laundry
living
counseling office
tele room
childrens play room
dining
daycare office
outdoor play

# LINCOLN—OMAHA, NEBRASKA

Although neither Lincoln nor Omaha has a visible homeless problem, in both cities there is tremendous demand for affordable housing. This demand, however, seems increasingly difficult to meet. Developing a clearer understanding of this problem was the primary goal of the Search for Shelter workshop.

A second goal was defining specific design problems to be addressed by architecture students at the University of Nebraska, Lincoln, in 1988.

The public forum took place in early November 1987, at which time housing and community development specialists shared their concerns. Sue Ellen Wall, chairperson of the Mayor's Task Force on Low-Income Housing, noted that homelessness is a problem in Lincoln even though the homeless themselves are not very visible. Here they are euphemistically called couch people—people who sleep on relatives' or friends' couches rather than in boxes or on grates on the street. And as in many cities, the number of people doubling or tripling up can be shockingly high.

Jim Cooke, of the Lincoln Housing Coalition, said that those participating in the design and programming phase must understand the needs of homeless people. Particularly important is "affordable privacy," such as offered in single-room-occupany hotels. Moreover, it is essential, he noted, to integrate the housing into the community at large.

At the public forum, the audience made several suggestions:
• make the housing flexible so that it can be used by the elderly, the young, or the handicapped, as well as able-bodied adults;
• change codes restricting the number of unrelated people who can live together to allow for group houses, housing that is particularly well suited for the chronically mentally ill and the elderly;
• redefine building and zoning codes to allow for the development of low-cost, long-term housing such as SROs and group homes;
• continue to educate the public about the special characteristics of homeless people;
• design buildings that do not have the

image of "project housing for the poor";
• investigate how the homeless can be involved in helping build their own shelters.

In the end, five projects were chosen for design and development by the student teams. The first project is the renovation of three warehouses into an SRO; the property is located in Lincoln's historic Haymarket warehouse district. For the second project another team will examine transitional housing for single parents with children, which can range from single detached houses on scattered sites or housing clustered together to share public spaces.

The third project is designing an addition to the Stephen Center in Omaha, a two-story building that formerly housed a commercial enterprise and now houses single men and women and families on an emergency basis. Renovating a basement into an apartment is the fourth project. The Lincoln Housing Program provided a low-interest loan to a Native American mother of two for the purchase of a single-family house. Renovation of the basement into an apartment will provide an essential source of income.

The last project involves a new design for an emergency shelter that puts a great deal of emphasis on supportive services, including detoxification and alcohol and drug rehabilitation.

CONTACT
Joan Higgins-Smith
University of Nebraska
Community and Regional Planning
    Department
Lincoln, Neb. 68588
(402) 472-3592

SPONSORS & PARTICIPANTS
Lincoln Chapter/AIA
Lincoln Housing Coalition
NHS of Lincoln
Omaha Chapter/AIA
Omaha Coalition for the Homeless
University of Nebraska at Lincoln
    Chapter/AIAS
University of Nebraska at Lincoln, College of Architecture. Faculty: Rick
    Kuhl, Ted A. Ertl

# ALBUQUERQUE, NEW MEXICO

Families that sink into homelessness in Albuquerque face a dire situation. The parents must choose between doubling up with another family, doling the children out to relatives, or trying to survive in emergency shelters, where most often they are separated. It is not surprising, then, that many families end up on the streets — living in tent cities, vacant buildings, or the family car. They simply have no other choice. The lucky ones are sent by the city welfare offices to shabby, low-rent motels.

This perilous plight of homeless families was discovered through extensive research by Albuquerque's Search for Shelter task force. Four students, a faculty advisor, and an architect and local AIA chapter member conducted interviews with shelter providers, care providers, and housing experts in the community. They studied the existing city, state, and federal programs helping the homeless, including legislation being considered by the Albuquerque City Council. The research team then mapped the location of shelters, other services for the homeless, and places where the homeless were known to "hang out." These findings would subsequently shape the scope of the task force's efforts.

Albuquerque has an estimated 800 to 1,200 homeless persons, the majority of whom are families, the chronically mentally ill, and single males. The 12 emergency shelters that exist offer scant counseling and rehabilitation services. In fact, shelter providers indicated that insufficient staffing and funding for such services are a more serious problem than insufficient emergency shelter.

Generally, gaining community acceptance for new shelters has been a difficult, and sometimes impossible, task for shelter providers. Although some programs adequately help the mentally ill and single males, there is little help for families. Therefore, the task force chose to redesign two facilities for homeless families — the Washington Apartments and the Eden Inn.

Located on a major thoroughfare in a city neighborhood and adjacent to a public park and a junior high school, the Washington Apartments seem an appropriate place to house families of three to five members. The apartment building fits into its neighborhood contextually. The interior, however, is badly dilapidated and in need of a complete renovation.

Since the building is listed in the National Register of Historic Places, virtually the entire exterior must be restored to its original appearance. (Exemptions from the rules are granted only when the occupants' safety is in question.) Generally speaking, the tax benefits gained in renovating a historically certified building outweigh the extra care needed to meet U.S. Department of Interior standards.

Another important financial source is federal government programs, monies designed to aid in housing homeless and low-income people. In the case of the Washington and the Eden, for example, it is crucial to know that the U.S. Department of Housing and Urban Development requires a two-room unit for families.

The Albuquerque Search for Shelter task force, therefore, chose as the basic unit a two-room suite with a kitchen-

East elevation

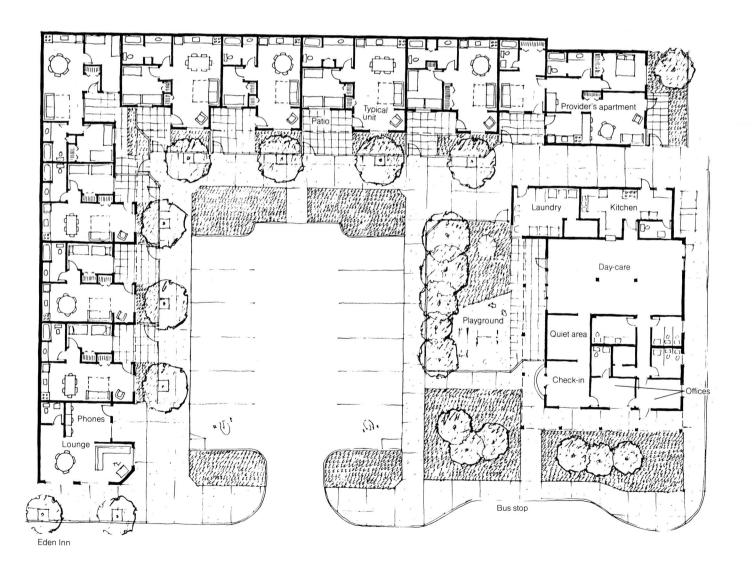

Eden Inn

Lounge

Phones

Patio

Typical unit

Provider's apartment

Laundry

Kitchen

Day-care

Playground

Quiet area

Check-in

Offices

Bus stop

ette and private bath. The parents would sleep on pullout beds in the living room. In all, 29 units would be created. The average minimum family stay would be 18 months, although there would be no time limit.

Careful attention was also paid to other basic needs of the guests. For example, such tight living quarters almost mandate adequate communal areas—both indoor and protected outdoor space—for day care, children's recreation, and adult recreational and social activities. Possible locations for such activities at the Washington Apartments are the courtyard spaces. The need for space for personal or job-related counseling was stressed.

Inadequate on-site parking is a major concern: There are only 11 spaces. Although a family would likely arrive at the Washington Apartments without a car, the task force estimated that within three to six months of employment a family could purchase one. But instead of carving out more parking spaces from the site, the design team suggested that placing a bus stop in front of the hotel would encourage the use of public transportation.

Overall, the Washington Apartments project would offer a homelike atmosphere that promotes a sense of self-worth, privacy as well as friendly connections and support, and a sense of belonging to the surrounding neighborhood.

To raise awareness and support for the Washington Apartments project, community members would be invited to join the complex's management board. They would also be asked to participate in the building's restoration, which is

envisioned as a joint public-private endeavor.

The Eden Inn would serve homeless families in a manner much different from the Washington Apartments. It would be smaller (eight units instead of 29), the length of stay would be much shorter (an average of one to six months instead of an unlimited time period), and its setting would be more rural.

In floor plan, the living arrangements would resemble those of the Washington Apartments—a two-room unit for each family, with private bath and pullout beds for the parents in the living room. Protected outdoor play areas, day care, and community spaces would be provided. Unlike the Washington Apartments, each unit would have a private outdoor patio.

Parking would not be a problem at the Eden Inn, which has space for 50 cars. And, even though the building is located on the outer edge of Albuquerque, a city bus line runs by the site so residents could take public transit. Surrounding the Eden are shops; a medical clinic is proposed next door.

Unlike the Washington, portions of the first floor of the Eden were once used as a restaurant. The design team proposed that the restaurant be retained to provide meals to residents and outsiders. It could also be used as a job-training facility for residents.

The Eden Inn's southwestern adobe style blends with that of surrounding buildings. The task force believes there would be little, if any, resistance to the project and that, in fact, the community would benefit from the renovation of the building and its subsequent upkeep.

*Drawings represent
creative development of
the Eden Inn, from
sketchy entrance study,
upper left, to the more
formal concept, middle
right.*

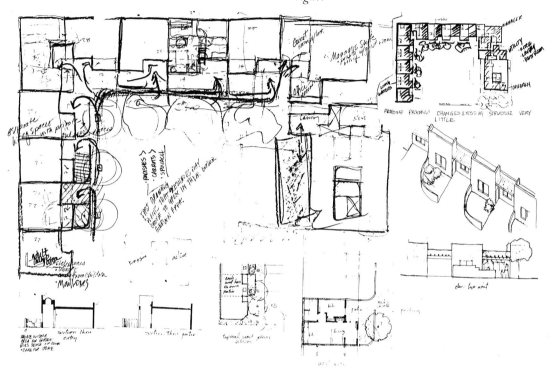

## PROJECT SIZE
(Washington Apartments)
Total area: 18,000 square feet
Residential spaces: 13,000 square feet
Common spaces: 400 square feet
Ancillary & circulation: 3,500 square
    feet
Number of units: 29
Number of beds: Variable

## COSTS
(Washington Apartments)
Building/land acquisition: $450,000
Renovation: $500,000 to $1 million

## PROJECT SIZE
(Eden Inn)
Total area: 8,300 square feet
Residential space: 5,800 square feet
Common space: 2,500 square feet
Number of units: 8
Number of beds: Variable

## COSTS
(Eden Inn)
Building/land acquisition: $500,000
Renovation: $250,000 to $800,000

## CONTACT
Joseph C. Brawley, AIA
Edward B. Norris, AIA
Design & Planning Assistance Center
University of New Mexico
120 Yale Boulevard, S.E.
Albuquerque, N.M. 87106
(505) 277-3647

## SPONSORS & PARTICIPANTS
Albuquerque Chapter/AIA
University of New Mexico, Design and
    Planning Assistance Center
University of New Mexico, School of
    Architecture and Planning
University of New Mexico Chapter/
    AIAS

# BROOKLYN, NEW YORK

Deliberately mixing different population groups in affordable, long- and short-term housing can be quite successful, with each group providing support or friendship for the others. In Brooklyn the Rose Kennedy Family Center will do just that by matching teenage mothers and the elderly. Plans were developed by architectural students in an advanced design studio at the Pratt Institute in conjunction with the Search for Shelter project and the New York chapter of Architects, Planners, and Designers for Social Responsibility.

The project involves the renovation of the top two floors of two buildings that had formerly been part of a Catholic school.

In the renovated school, permanent housing in the form of 20 studio apartments would be available for the elderly; the teenagers would be housed in 10 semiprivate units clustered around a central lounge. The teenagers and their children would also have access to a family dining room, laundry room, and children's playroom.

As a stepping stone from dependent to independent living, four self-sufficient "training" apartments would be available to the guests. Permanent housing would be the goal, with the nonprofit group sponsoring the project, Project Teen Aid, helping to locate a guest's future permanent housing.

The elderly will be encouraged to develop foster-grandparent relationships with the teens and their children. The design will facilitate this interaction through the inclusion of shared spaces, such as elevator lobbies and circulation spaces.

Appropriate social services will be provided to both populations. The courtyard will provide recreation space. A day-care facility for 30 to 40 children, for both the children in the shelter and those in the greater community, will likely lessen community opposition to the facility.

Whether the parish will maintain possession of the schools or whether Project Teen Aid will purchase the property has not yet been determined; Project Teen Aid will be the operator. Possible sources of funding for acquisition and renovation include New York State's Homeless Housing Assistance Program and its Housing Trust Fund and Rehousing Assistance Program and New York City's Capital Budget Homeless Housing Program. Operational funds for the transitional housing will be provided by New York City's Human Resources Administration. The elderly residents' rent will be covered by their state shelter allowance.

## PROJECT SIZE

Total area: 42,830 square feet
Residential spaces: 16,200 square feet
Common spaces: 6,234 square feet
Ancillary and circulation: 14,396 square feet
Day care facility: 5,000 square feet
Classrooms: 1,150 square feet
Number of units: 34
Number of beds: 57
Staff apartments: 2 to 6 persons

## COSTS

Construction: $3.5 million
Soft costs: $450,000
Acquisition: Not available

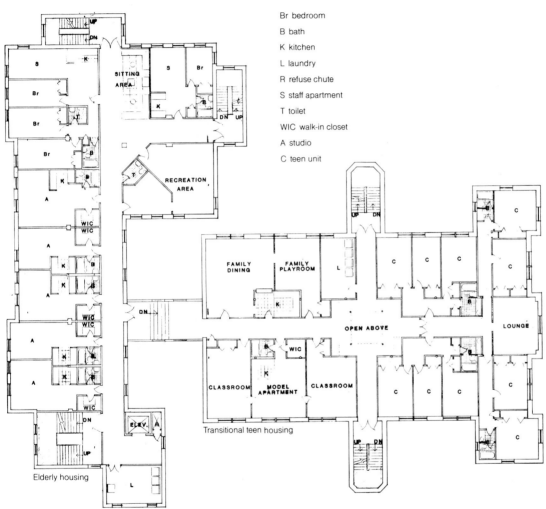

Br bedroom
B bath
K kitchen
L laundry
R refuse chute
S staff apartment
T toilet
WIC walk-in closet
A studio
C teen unit

SITTING AREA

RECREATION AREA

FAMILY DINING

FAMILY PLAYROOM

OPEN ABOVE

LOUNGE

CLASSROOM

MODEL APARTMENT

CLASSROOM

Transitional teen housing

Elderly housing

Second floor

CONTACT
Cindy Harden
Pratt Architectural Center
Pratt Institute
379 DeKalb Avenue
Brooklyn, N.Y. 11205
(718) 636-3486

SPONSORS & PARTICIPANTS
Brooklyn Catholic Charities Housing
    Office: Cathy Herman
Catholic Charities: Sister Maureen Carey
Carroll Kowal: Social Services Consultant
Pratt Architectural Collaborative, Pratt
    Institute Center for Community and
    Environmental Development: Cindy
    Harden, Robert Santoriello.
Pratt Institute, School of Architecture.
    Students: Betty Capehart, Janice Kel-
    ler, Camil Malouf, Luis Nieves.
    Faculty: Christine Bevington
Pratt Institute Chapter/AIA
Project Teen Aid: Sister Sally Butler
Peter Woll Architects: Chuck Brome

# ITHACA, NEW YORK

Like other small communities around the country, Ithaca has only recently acknowledged a growing problem of homelessness. The official count is only 50 to 75 "known" homeless in the city; unofficial counts of homeless or housing-vulnerable people are much higher.

In June 1986 the county mental health services board called on the non-profit holding organization HOMES, Inc., to chair a public hearing on the housing options available to homeless people. It quickly became evident that the chronically mentally ill were the most vulnerable population in Ithaca to regional mental health care cutbacks. But other factors contributing to homelessness were acknowledged—ones that ultimately could bring others into the ranks of the homeless; most significant among these is the one percent vacancy rate for apartments in the city.

As a result of these meetings, representatives of service and charitable organizations began to develop concepts for a minimally supervised SRO. This committee then turned to Cornell University for student interns for technical services. In fact, interns from the school of architecture, school of city and regional planning, and preservation planners have been providing such services to the Ithaca Neighborhood Housing Services for six years. The interns would help draft and design, make surveys and maps assessing neighborhood needs, and provide historical documentation.

This approach did encounter some problems. The city's adoption of stricter building codes made it virtually impossible to build without the services of a licensed architect. At the same time,

fewer licensed architects were willing to face liability risks unless they were more closely involved in the projects.

The dilemma was temporarily solved when Phil Handler, AIA, an architect and member of the AIA Housing Committee, began to set up a Search for Shelter workshop in Ithaca. The project would be an SRO for 18 single adults (18 to 55 years old). It would offer 24-hour supervision and minimal support services, one meal per day, linen service and on-site laundry facilities, medication supervision as necessary, and an in-house, "caring" manager. There would be recreational and leisure space indoors, while the back yard would provide protected, outdoor space.

The building under study (and previously purchased by HOMES, Inc., is a two-story frame house. Originally designed to house a single family, it had been converted 10 years ago to a group home for college students.

The team's proposal called for a two-story addition to the building, placed at the rear of the original house to minimize bulk and to obtain neighborhood support. Its style echoes that of the original; in fact, from a distance it would be hard to differentiate the old from the new. The addition would house 14. Because SROs are not defined in the Ithaca zoning and building codes, variances were necessary.

Construction of the addition and renovation of the existing Green Street house was originally planned for summer 1988. The construction will be managed by Ithaca Neighborhood Housing Services. After completion, it will be managed by the nonprofit HOMES, Inc. A capital grant will be provided

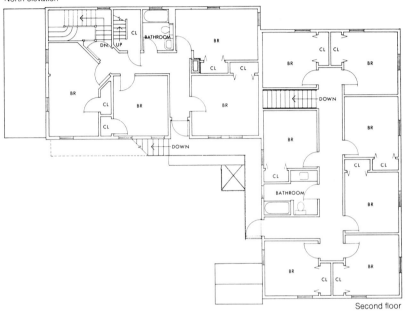

North elevation

Second floor

by the New York State Homeless Housing and Assistance Program. Operating money will be sought from the New York State Department of Social Services. Addition monies will be raised locally by HOMES, Inc.

## PROJECT SIZE

Total area: 5,000 square feet
Residential spaces: 2,000 square feet
Common spaces: 1,600 square feet
Ancillary & circulation: 1,250 square feet
Other: 150 square feet
Number of units: 18
Number of beds: 18

## COSTS

Hard acquisition costs: $83,000
Soft acquisition costs: $20,000
Construction (minor rehabilitation of existing building & construction of addition): $222,000
TOTAL: $325,000

## CONTACT

Ben Curtis
Rehabilitation Coordinator
Ithaca Neighborhood Housing Services
520 West Green Street
Ithaca, N.Y. 14850
(607) 277-4500

## SPONSORS & PARTICIPANTS

Cornell University, Department of Architecture
Cornell University, Preservation Planners
Cornell University, School of City and Regional Planning
Cornell University Chapter/AIAS
Ithaca Chapter/AIA
Ithaca NHS, Inc.

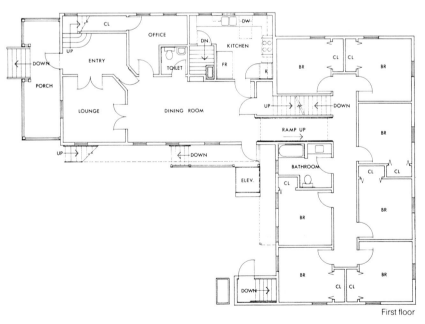

First floor

The Green Street House

# NEW YORK, NEW YORK

Conceived for a design studio at City College Architectural Center, at the City University of New York, this project involves the development and reconstruction of housing in the Cooper Square urban renewal area. In broad terms the project addresses the changing nature of urban housing and how these changes affect the inhabitants and their needs, the forms of the housing and management, and other services (if offered).

The Search for Shelter task force stated the project's guiding philosophy: "The semipublic and public extensions of the home from streets to open space, shared facilities, neighborhood services, etc., are becoming more complexly integrated into the residential domain, as are all significant elements that expand and challenge the personal experience of the home. User groups of housing have changed: Economic and social pressures have created new types of households—single-parent families, unrelated young adults, and intergenerational groups—whose spatial needs are often quite different from those of the traditional nuclear family, for whom dwellings are usually designed. The providers of housing have changed too, as has the context for housing production."

For the two-block area in the Bowery, boarded by East 2nd Street, Second Avenue, Houston Street, and Bowery Street, the following are the design requirements:
• provide affordable housing for the surrounding community (mainly artists) and for homeless people;
• explore what new dwelling types might adequately house the homeless and establish a spatial order for these units as well as for the entire block;
• determine how to integrate space for economic and social services and recreation;
• develop affordable housing that can remain affordable;
• respect the social base of the larger neighborhood and the spatial organization of existing blocks while creating a new order.

Building types to be included are large apartments with multiple bathrooms and shared cooking-eating-leisure spaces, dwellings with workspace (such as personal office, a studio, or a small day care center), and apartments for single-parent households or to be shared by the young and the elderly.

The project was broken into several phases: neighborhood and zoning analysis, a field visit, program development, a site plan, and schematic designs. The 22,000 square feet of commercial space is to include specialized Bowery stores, a convenience store, space for job-training workshops, artisan studios, and garden spaces. Shared facilities are to total 17,000 square feet for a day-care center, an adult care center, health-related facilities, social services for homeless women, and educational programs. To create this community of artisans, artists, low-income residents, and relocated homeless families, 263,000 square feet of residential space is to be designed as traditional units (efficiencies and one-, two-, and three-bedroom units) and as nontraditional units.

Based on suggestions from the Search for Shelter workshop, a community named Extra Place will eventually be developed under the auspices of the Cooper Square Community Organization.

*Above, design by C. Willy Zambrano calls for an SRO for transitional housing to be mixed with low-cost apartments.*

CONTACT
Ghislaine Hermanuz
City College Architectural Center
Convent Avenue at 138th Street
New York, N.Y. 10031
(212) 690-6751

SPONSORS & PARTICIPANTS
City College Architectural Center
City College, School of Architecture,
    City University of New York
City College Chapter/AIAS
Cooper Square Community Organization

# SYRACUSE, NEW YORK

Although the reported 540 homeless people in Syracuse seems small when compared with the populations of other cities, the 10,000 households believed to be housing vulnerable loom much more menacingly. It seems quite appropriate, then, that the Syracuse Search for Shelter task group chose as its project the renovation of an existing SRO hotel and at the same time chose not to displace permanently the building's current residents.

In question is the six-story Snowdon apartment building, once one of the city's most elegant residences. Built in 1902, its brick and stone exterior is still in generally good condition. The interior, however, is quite deteriorated and does not comply with current building codes. The building currently houses about 200 people. Because it is located close to downtown, the Snowdon seems a prime target for conversion to luxury apartments or offices or demolition.

The Syracuse Common Council Task Force on the Homeless and Housing Vulnerable suggested the Snowdon as a possible project. The task was clearly stated: Bring the interior up to code while significantly improving the quality of its spaces and renovate the building without causing the dislocation of current residents.

The latter requirement proved easy to satisfy. Renovation could be done in phases, the Search for Shelter team suggested; temporary housing could be provided off site for the residents affected.

Early on it was decided that although the renovated Snowdon would be primarily for single men, the spaces should be easily adapted for women or couples. The ruling philosophy is "to create a non-institutional, residential environment with opportunities for as much privacy or socialization as each individual may require," according to Peter J. Arsenault, AIA. Socialization among the guests would be promoted by locating common eating areas on each floor and a large communal space on the main floor for dining, recreation, educational or group activities. Social services—job counseling, mental health counseling, medical care, legal assistance, religious services, and others—would be offered on a rotating basis in the building.

Most units would be efficiencies; some would be suites. The interior service courtyard would become the major enclosed communal space on the first floor. Some first-floor units would be turned into social service rooms.

The neighboring residents have endorsed the project as "important to the neighborhood since it prevents displacement of residents and serves a need for low-income housing."

In the end, the most difficult issues for the task force to resolve were how the renovation will be funded, who will purchase the building, and who will operate it. The cost to acquire and renovate the Snowdon, in accordance with the Search for Shelter team's plan, is an estimated $3 million to $4 million. Funding, Arsenault says, is likely to come from state and city sources—such as the New York State Homeless Housing Assistance Program, the New York State Housing Trust Fund, the New York State Affordable Housing Program, and the City of Syracuse Department of Community Development or from funds generated by the Homeless Assistance Act of 1987—or funding from

*Exterior courtyard would become an indoor two-story common room.*

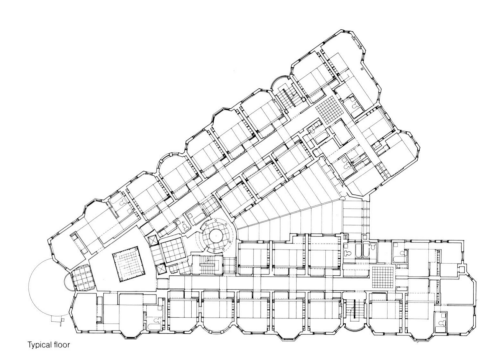

Typical floor

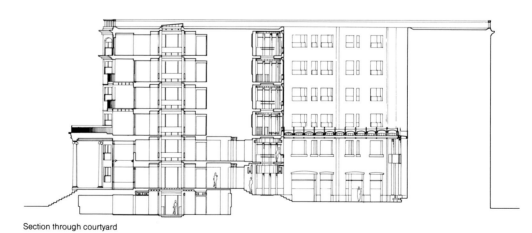

Section through courtyard

the U.S. Department of Housing and Urban Development programs. Operation, management, and services will likely be funded through rental income (some of which is paid for by social service agencies, churches, or other charitable organizations).

CONTACT
Peter J. Arsenault, AIA
4911 Yeaworth Lane
Manilus, N.Y. 13104
(315) 474-1714

SPONSORS & PARTICIPANTS
Peter J. Arsenault, Architect
Catholic Charities
Central New York Chapter/AIA
Church of the Savior
First English Lutheran Church

NEHDA, Inc., (Northeast Hauley Development Association)
NHS of Syracuse, Inc.
Onondaga County Department of Social Services
Palucci Engineering PC, Roberto Palucci
Dennis Spina, AIA
Syracuse Blueprint Company, Inc.
Syracuse Common Council Task Force on the Homeless and Housing Vulnerable
Syracuse University, School of Architecture. Students: Don Argus, Alejandro Ceppi, Lee Cravey, Christine Dewey, Edward Duffy, Adam Lane, David Levy, Jeff O'Brien, Chris Sapara-Grant, Jeff Snedecker. Faculty: Bruce Coleman, Roberto Pachon, Lee Temple
Syracuse University Chapter/AIAS
Urban Ministry

# CINCINNATI, OHIO

The rallying cry behind the Cincinnati Search for Shelter effort was that decent housing must be found for low-income and homeless individuals and families. As University of Cincinnati professor of architecture David L. Niland put it, "Most of our low-income housing ends up providing only a subsistence environment—people are warmed and fed, but the environment is an insult to human dignity. And I'm not talking about an abstract concept of human dignity—I'm not talking gold leaf. I'm talking light, air, no roaches or rats. I've seen jails that have greater appeal and ambience than most of the public housing in this country."

In an attempt to define specific housing needs of the homeless and low-income in Cincinnati, the Search for Shelter task group, under the direction of the Community Planning and Design Center, sponsored a daylong event. Activities included speakers, panel discussions, and a two-hour design charrette. Seventy-two persons attended—federal, state, and local housing experts, homeless service providers, representatives of civic groups, shelter providers, architects, planners, students, and interested members of the community.

Keynote speakers and panelists offered the following insights:
• Barbara Poppe-Smith, co-chairperson of the Greater Cincinnati Homeless Coalition dispelled the myth that the estimated 16,000 homeless persons in the Cincinnati area are homeless by choice. Among the factors she cited for their involuntary homeless state are domestic strife, alcoholism, mental illness, and unemployment. What is needed, she said, is more permanent housing that is safe, sanitary, affordable, and nondiscriminatory.
• Buddy Gray, director of the Drop-Inn Center Shelter House in Cincinnati, suggested three ways the public could help the homeless: (1) work soup lines and provide cleaning, maintenance, and renovation of buildings; (2) donate food, money, and material goods; and (3) advocate the rights and privileges homeless people deserve as human beings.
• Harris Forusz, professor at the school of planning at the University of Cincinnati, maintained that Americans should look to European countries and how they provide government-assisted housing. "The United States government is some 30 to 40 years behind the Europeans, who devote large portions of their national budgets to public housing," he suggested.
• David J. Allor, professor at the school of planning, University of Cincinnati, proposed a "systems view of shelter" that offers three classes of services—shelter, human services, and functional training. Shelter should include emergency, transitional, and permanent housing. Human services include medical, dental, social-psychological, welfare, and other assistance. Training should consist of literacy, job training, and what he terms "urban survival skills."

During the workshop's design session, seven teams addressed the design problems of three shelters that exist in the community and are in need of renovation or unit reconfiguration. The housing to be developed is mainly for women and children, although some units are to accommodate singles and families. Transitional to long-term housing needs were addressed, and particularly

View looking north

Third floor kitchen

*Several views of ANAWIM Housing, Inc., transitional housing for singles and families.*

Entry hall

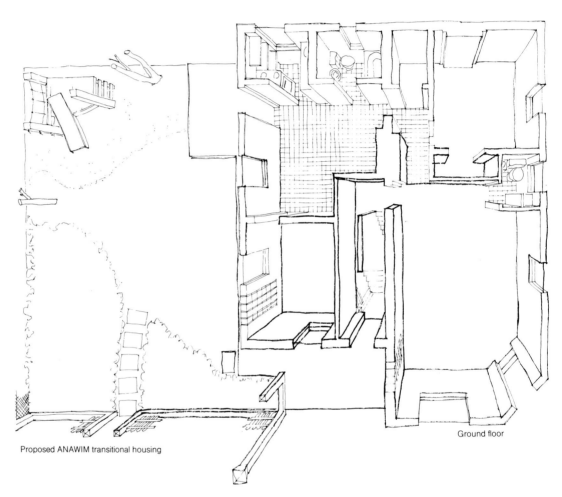

Proposed ANAWIM transitional housing

Ground floor

applauded was shelter that lends itself to independent living.

Basically, the design solutions can be divided into three categories: (1) minimal alteration—cosmetic work such as replastering and painting; (2) moderate alteration—scaling down room partitions and dividers to allow the introduction of natural light into each unit; and (3) extensive alteration—unit reconfiguration in which demolition of walls would permit new design solutions. The focus of the workshop was a building in Newport, Ky., owned by the ANAWIM Housing, Inc. (transitional housing) and two buildings in Cincinnati owned by the Franciscan Home Development, Inc. (permanent housing). Although not provided on any of the sites, social services would be available within three blocks of each project.

Currently, Cincinnati does not have a plan of action to meet the needs of the homeless, although a blueprint of housing needs for greater Cincinnati is being developed. It is hoped that the Search for Shelter efforts and continued interest by the Search for Shelter members will be the catalyst necessary to implement that blueprint.

PROJECT SIZE
(ANAWIM Housing, Inc.)
2,750 square feet

COSTS
(ANAWIM Housing, Inc.)
Property acquisition: $20,000
Materials & skilled labor: $24,000
Insurance: $850
Utilities: $600
Miscellaneous: $500
Repayment of loans: $1,500
TOTAL: $47,450

PROJECT SIZE
(Franciscan Home Development, Inc.)
420 East 12th Street: 4,680 square feet
424 East 12th Street: 3,216 square feet

COSTS
(Both buildings unless indicated)
General construction: $52,800
Plumbing improvements: $16,000
New wiring: $14,000
New windows (424 E. 12th): $8,000
Tuck pointing & exterior painting (420
    E. 12th): $5,000
Tuck pointing (424 E. 12th): $2,000
Roof repair: $2,200
TOTAL: $100,000

CONTACT
Eric J. Russo
Community Planning and Design
    Center
University of Cincinnati
Cincinnati, Ohio 45221
(513) 475-4943

SPONSORS & PARTICIPANTS
Cincinnati Department of Buildings and
    Inspections: Gregory Nicholls, AIA
Cincinnati Department of Neighbor-
hood Housing and Conservation:
    Gerard Hyland
Cincinnati Human Services: Barry
    Schwartz
Cincinnati Metropolitan Housing
    Authority: Neil Blunt
Community Planning and Design Cen-
    ter, University of Cincinnati: Duraid
    Da'as, Eric J. Russo
Drop-Inn Center Shelter House: Buddy
    Gray
Greater Cincinnati Homeless Coalition:
    Barbara Poppe-Smith
HUD: Norman Deas
Jones & Speer Architects: Jose Garcia,
    Ken Jones, James Kalsbeek
Miami (of Ohio) University
Provident Bank
Robert Sala, AIA
Savings and Loan Association of South-
    western Ohio: Roderick Greene
Smith Stevens Young: Don Stevens
University of Cincinnati, Architecture
    Department. Faculty: David Niland,
    Richard Stevens
University of Cincinnati, School of Plan-
    ning. Faculty: David J. Allor, Harris
    Forusz
University of Cincinnati Chapter/AIAS
U.S. Jaycees, local branch

# PHILADELPHIA, PENNSYLVANIA

*Patricia McLaughlin, 32, lives in a small room at the Mid-City YWCA with her four children, aged 5 to 9, amid roaches, peeling paint, and gouged walls. But things could be worse. "I'd be living on the streets, probably, if I didn't have this," she said. Things could also be better at the 63-year-old YWCA, located in the 2000 block of Chestnut Street, where McLaughlin is one of the more than 200 homeless women and 100 children who come through the YWCA's emergency shelter each year.* — The Philadelphia Inquirer *(Nov. 16, 1987).*

To the Search for Shelter task force it was obvious that the YWCA's Crozier Residence for Women would greatly benefit from some design attention. Located in an eight-story, 148,566-square-foot facility, the residence houses from 100 to 125 women and their children. Other activities in the building include the YWCA's programs, nursery school, and offices. Rooms are too small for long-term living. The atmosphere is institutional and storage space and ventilation is inadequate. No common areas or outdoor recreation space exist, and kitchens are too small.

The program set up by the YWCA called for emergency, transitional, and permanent housing. For each type of housing, the YWCA required efficiency and one- and two-bedroom units, each unit with a private bath and some built-in furniture. For common areas, the YWCA's wish list included cooking and dining areas for six to 12 persons, children's playrooms, laundry rooms, community spaces, a library, offices for support staff, storage facilities, vending areas, a first-aid station, and quiet areas.

The team from Spring Garden College explored ways of making a variety of spaces, public as well as semiprivate. The top floors—the sixth and the seventh—would be reserved for mothers with children, and the roof of the building would be transformed into an outdoor playground. Permanent living quarters would have small kitchenettes to enable independent living.

Two floor plans were developed. The first calls for open communal dining-kitchen spaces across from an open lounge. These would allow for natural lighting and cross ventilation in the corridor. The first plan would allow a greater housing capacity than the second, but the second would provide more privacy. Recessed entries would become porchlike niches for the clustered units in an effort to relieve the tunnel-corridor arrangement.

CONTACT
Jim Wentling, AIA
260 South Broad
Philadelphia, Pa. 19102
(215) 735-0038

SPONSORS & PARTICIPANTS
Drexel University, Department of
 Architecture
Drexel University Chapter/AIAS
Mid-City YWCA
Philadelphia Chapter/AIA
Philadelphia College of Arts
Spring Garden College
Spring Garden College Chapter/AIAS
Temple University, Division of
 Architecture
Temple University Chapter/AIAS
University of Pennsylvania, Department
 of Architecture
Jim Wentling, AIA

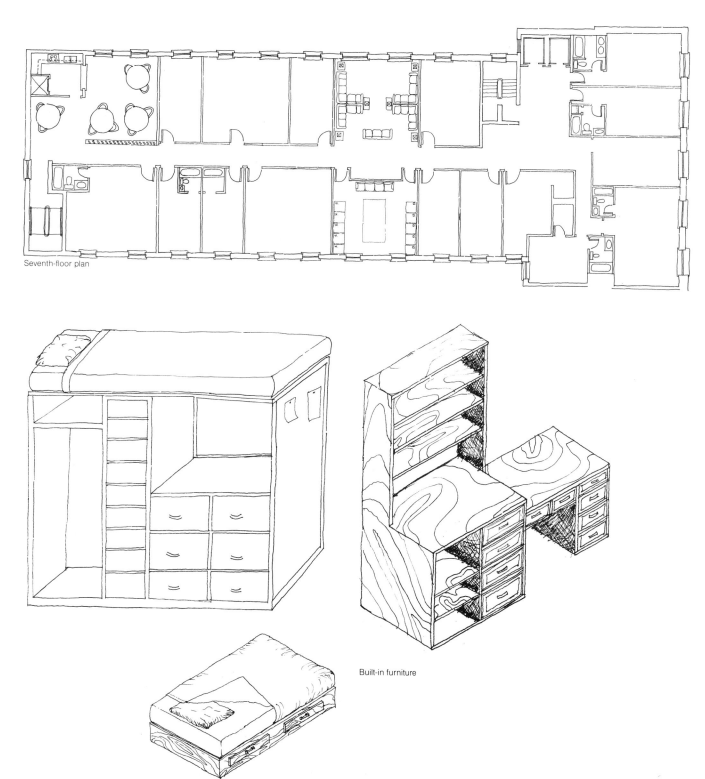

Seventh-floor plan

Built-in furniture

# PITTSBURGH, PENNSYLVANIA

Early on, the Pittsburgh Search for Shelter task force chose to work with existing shelter providers to identify real housing needs. In the end, the five task force teams worked with five shelter providers. The projects ranged from an emergency shelter for homeless men to a shelter for battered women and children. And while the building types for the shelters varied, the philosophical problem was the same: Should the shelter look like a home, a hotel, or what? A description of each follows.

*Womansplace.* Refuge for battered women and their children is scarce in parts of Pittsburgh. In the Womansplace shelter, housing and comfort would be offered for up to 30 days, while they searched for more permanent accommodations. Support services would be available. "We have worked with battered women for 11 years and we realize that a lack of self-confidence and self-esteem is one common characteristic," says a staff member. "For them to take any action, support and information about what is available are needed."

A warm, homelike atmosphere is essential to help heal the emotional wounds of the residents. Both a sense of community and of security and privacy are offered—through communal living and dining spaces and private bedrooms.

The shelter would occupy a renovated doctor's office and residence. Any additions would maintain the residential qualities of the building. The scale, materials, and image would reflect those of the surrounding neighborhood. In the renovation the former office and storage spaces would be converted into staff space and the former living quarters into the shelter residents' rooms.

The first floor and basement areas would be solely for support services for the shelter residents—spaces for private counseling, a children's play area, and offices for the staff and volunteers.

Funding for the project will be sought from HUD (under the Homeless Assistance Act of 1987), Federal Emergency Management Agency funds, Community Development Block grants, state funds, low-interest loans, foundation grants, and private donations.

*Light of Life Rescue Mission.* The acquisition by the Light of Life Rescue Mission of the neighboring Moose Lodge would allow for 110 additional units. In effect, a vertical hierarchy would be established: The transient homeless would be housed dormitory style in the basement; those requiring bridge housing—i.e., those in transition from homelessness to being housed on a more permanent basis—would be on the second floor in four- and two-men rooms; and individuals on the third floor would be in more permanent SRO units. The existing rescue mission building could then house women and children.

The Moose Lodge would also house administrative offices, counseling offices, conference rooms, and classrooms. There would be a recreation lounge, quiet lounge, and a library, all for use by the bridge-housing and SRO tenants.

Other design characteristics include:
• creating a sense of home and sharing within the facility;
• creating comfortably scaled sleeping rooms similar in feel to a typical bedroom in a single-family house;
• providing individual entries and a win-

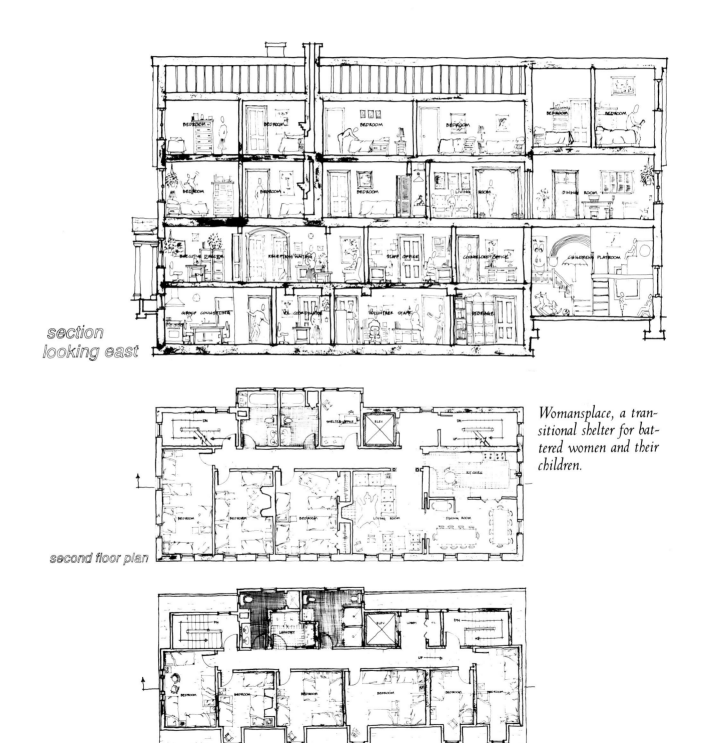

*section looking east*

*second floor plan*

*third floor plan*

Womansplace, a transitional shelter for battered women and their children.

79

*The Governor Hotel (center left) and its street scene.*

# PROPOSED FIRST FLOOR PLAN

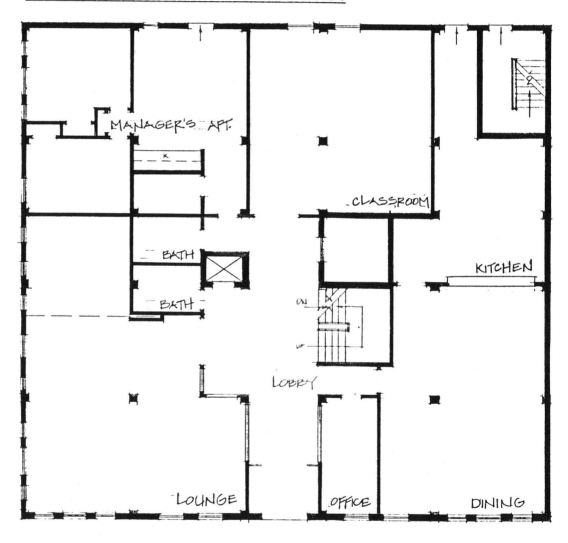

MANAGER'S APT.

BATH

BATH

CLASSROOM

KITCHEN

LOBBY

LOUNGE

OFFICE

DINING

dow for each bedroom;
• encouraging interaction among residents by the inclusion of communal social areas;
• defining a strong linear progression at the transient dormitory entrance (to allow minimal staffing while providing maximum observation of the guests);
• maximizing the use of the existing courtyard for social events;
• providing a covered entrance to the transient dormitory and dining areas as a way of extending the hierarchy of spatial enclosure from outside to inside.

*East End Cooperative Ministry.* The services of the East End Cooperative Ministry are many: an emergency shelter for homeless men, a bridge-housing program that provides support for those able to make the transition from homelessness to self support, respite housing for those recovering from an illness or surgery, and a program to help poor families and individuals who are on the brink of homelessness.

To serve these four populations, the renovation of the dilapidated Governor Hotel was proposed. The design team was asked to provide decent housing and support services for 39 homeless men capable of self-sufficiency, three persons in need of respite care, 26 single persons, and six households of one or two adults and two to four children.

The hotel is located in East Liberty, which was the focus of an urban renewal project in the 1960s that failed to bring new life to this part of Pittsburgh. The area is now experiencing a revitalization, however, as two new shopping centers are being built. The Governor Hotel is seen as a vital part of this revitalization effort.

The Governor Hotel was built in 1880 with four floors and a basement. Around the turn of the century, two floors were added to the top, increasing the total square footage to 23,250. Constructed of steel columns and beams with clay tile waffle slabs, the building is structurally sound. An elevator shaft exists in the center of the building.

There are 75 single rooms and 50 bathrooms, some private and others shared by two rooms. The existing arrangement of rooms seems conducive to reuse, thus saving the cost of demolishing the old walls and building new ones. Rooms for respite care require private baths; single men could easily share bathrooms.

To familiarize themselves with the future users of the hotel, the Search for Shelter team members spent time at the existing shelter and served lunch at its soup kitchen. There they found enthusiasm among the guests, particularly the men, to participate in the demolition and cleanup of the Governor.

In the redesign, the second floor would contain two types—respite care and bridge-housing rooms—as well as a day room where respite care guests could socialize in an atmosphere quieter than that of the main lounge. The third through sixth floors would contain single rooms for homeless men and apartments for families. In all, 69 units would be created. Throughout the building, new plumbing, heating, sprinkler, and electrical systems would be added, as well as new windows, roof, and elevator.

*Holy Trinity House.* The philosophy behind the Holy Trinity House is explained by Rev. William Whitworth, the pastor of Holy Trinity: "To give a man a fish is to keep him hungry, but to teach him to fish is to give him life." The shelter, therefore, encourages residents to seek employment and offers services to help them in their pursuit.

The premise can also be stated as follows: The ability to relate to a large group of people is essential if the shelterless person desires reestablishment in society. The role of the communal space, then, becomes very important in structuring an environment. The question then becomes: Should the shelter force communal interaction or provide people with a chance to participate in group activities? The design team felt it should simply provide a choice.

Currently, Trinity House is inefficiently used. The ground floor serves as a church for 200 parishioners, the second floor houses 18 homeless persons, and the basement contains a soup kitchen. Renovation would be accomplished in two stages.

In the first phase the existing environment would be improved by using more homey exterior and interior finishes, relocating the shelter entrance, enlarging the soup kitchen and food storage, providing space for chapel receptions, and repairing all mechanical systems. In the second phase the program and its environment would be restructured. In the basement would be the skill-building center and family units. On the first floor would be the job center and rehabilitation classrooms, the soup kitchen and dining hall, secured access to the second floor and basement, and new communal spaces located off the main circulation path. On the second floor, the number and quality of bedrooms would be increased.

*Pleasant Valley Shelter.* The shelter is located in the Northside section of Pittsburgh, a primarily low-income community where homeowners struggle for improvements in the physical quality of buildings and the overall image of the community. The shelter is opposed by those residents.

The shelter currently exists in the basement of the Pleasant Valley Church, a space that formerly served the church's community center. It serves 20 to 24 men. The main objectives are to provide overnight shelter, two meals, and showering and laundry facilities.

Individual counseling, designed to help guide the men towards reintegration into society, is an important function of the shelter. This counseling is directed toward strengthening self-esteem and self-respect, rehabilitating residents of drug and alcohol problems, and giving direction concerning welfare and financial aid programs.

The Search for Shelter design team concluded that physical improvements should be directed toward meeting essential functional needs of the shelter— specifically, the lighting, ventilation, acoustic insulation, visual control, spatial organization, and structural integrity.

Other improvements would be replacement of the building's internal structure; the addition of overhead fluorescent lights; and replacement of tinted glass with transparent.

In addition, the Pleasant Valley Shelter would be improved by creating a more comfortable and usable lounge, moving the storage area to increase sleeping and lounge spaces, introducing new private spaces for counseling, and converting second-floor space into offices.

PROJECT SIZE
(The Governor Hotel)
Total area: 23,250 square feet
Number of units: 69

COSTS
(The Governor Hotel)
General construction: $1,176,481
Contingencies: $47,059
Architect's fee: $94,118

PROJECT SIZE
(Light of Life Rescue Mission)
Total area: 42,800 square feet
Original building: 19,670 square feet
Moose building: 23,130 square feet
Number of units: 110
One dormitory: 50 beds
12 bridge-housing units: 48 beds
Single-room-occupancy units: 12 beds

PROJECT SIZE
(Womansplace)
Total area: 8,778 square feet
Residential: 2,574 square feet
Common space: 1,047 square feet
Work spaces: 2,557 square feet
Ancillary & circulation: 3,600 square
    feet
Number of units: 9
Number of beds: 35

COSTS
(Womansplace)
Renovation: $350,000

CONTACT
Thomas Celli, AIA
Celli, Flynn & Associates
931 Pennsylvania Avenue
Pittsburgh, Pa. 15222
(412) 281-9400

SPONSORS & PARTICIPANTS
Burt Hill Kosar Rittelmann Associates:
    Naomi Yoran, AIA
Carnegie Mellon University, Department
    of Architecture. Students: David Arai,
    Clark Brewer, David Celento, Maria
    Cole, Annalisa Edbladh, Steve
    Gibson, David Goff, Greg Knoop,
    Aaron Levin, Audrey Liu, Michael
    McDonnell, Scott Mulrooney, Shelly
    Pressley, Jim Rauth, Elizabeth
    Rexrode, Raphy Rosner, Betsy Smith.
    Faculty: Omer Akin, Stefanie
    Ledowitz
Carnegie Mellon University Chapter/
    AIAS
Celli, Flynn & Associates: Thomas Celli,
    AIA, Stephen Pacey
East End Cooperative Ministry: George
    Steffey
IKM-SGE Architects: Fred Watts, AIA
Light of Life Rescue Mission, Inc.:
    William Quigley
MacLachlan Cornelius & Filoni
    Architects: Louisa Grauel, Alan
    Hohlfelder, AIA, Claire Wallace Kist
Pleasant Valley Shelter: John Kulevich,
    Rev. John Scotland
Pittsburgh Chapter/AIA: Lana Andrews
Trinity House: Rev. William Whitworth
University of Pittsburgh, Graduate
    School of Public and International
    Affairs
Urban League of Pittsburgh: Leon
    Haley
Williams Trebilcock Whitehead
    Architects: Dan Delisio, Glen
    Schultz, AIA
Womansplace: Valerie Tutokey

# KNOXVILLE, TENNESSEE

On any given day in Knoxville there are 250 to 300 homeless persons, according to the Knoxville Coalition for the Homeless; during any given month the total number of homeless is approximately 1,000. And while shelter opportunities are generally adequate, support services are not. What is needed, says the Knoxville Coalition for the Homeless, is a center that would coordinate available support services with the needs of the homeless—persons living both in and out of shelters. Ready to undertake that task is the Volunteer Ministry Center.

A nonprofit organization established in 1976, the Volunteer Ministry Center (previously called Volunteer Helpers) currently houses 25 persons in single rooms, 34 persons in overnight emergency shelter, and 12 resident staff members. The center also serves 150 meals daily in two adjoining buildings. When renovated, the center would provide emergency housing only when other shelters are filled to capacity. Instead, its main role would be to coordinate services and referrals for the homeless. Staff housing and some transitional housing would be offered.

The Volunteer Ministry Center would provide two types of services: (1) basic support such as referrals, meals, day rooms, and an outdoor gathering space and (2) in-depth case management. To keep these two service centers autonomous, the design team created two separate entrances.

The Drop-in Center would be located off Gay Street (a major city artery) and would have a side entrance. This arrangement would minimize the clusters and lines of shelter guests on Gay Street and, in the process, somewhat dilute neighborhood opposition. The Gay Street storefronts would then be used by specific service providers for case management. Maintaining the storefront image was also seen as important in diminishing neighborhood resistance.

Resistance to the center has been strong, particularly under the previous management, but that hard resistance is now softening because of the Volunteer Ministry Center approach. For instance, the Search for Shelter workshop participants learned that neighboring merchants and developers "appear to have accepted the shelter as part of the area," according to Emily Freeman of the East Tennessee Community Design Center. "They realize that the homeless will remain in the area whether the shelter is there or not, and they have suggested ways for the shelter to improve its appearance and services."

In the redesign, common spaces —both indoor and outdoor—were given special emphasis: lounges and social rooms with a familial setting in the Drop-In Center, a private lounge for resident staff, and a sheltered deck and the reuse of a currently neglected courtyard as controlled outdoor spaces. Substantial renovation would be needed to bring both of the adjoining buildings up to code requirements.

The Volunteer Ministry Center owns and operates the building. It will receive city funding for renovation of the facade and construction of a new fire stair. HUD funding and revenues from the Episcopal Diocese of East Tennessee and other churches are being sought to complete the renovation, estimated at $500,000.

Volunteer Ministry Center

Patio
Dining room
Entry
Kitchen
Reception
Director
Storage
Staff lounge
Offices
Conference room
Street level

## PROJECT SIZE
Residential spaces: 22,000 square feet
Courtyard: 1,500 square feet
Common spaces: 4,000 square feet
Case management/reception:
  3,800 square feet

## CONTACT
Emily Freeman
East Tennessee Community Design
  Center
1522 Highland Avenue
Knoxville, Tenn. 37916
(615) 525-9945

## SPONSORS & PARTICIPANTS
East Tennessee Community Design
  Center
East Tennessee Chapter/AIA
University of Tennessee at Knoxville,
  School of Architecture
University of Tennessee Chapter/AIAS

# DALLAS, TEXAS

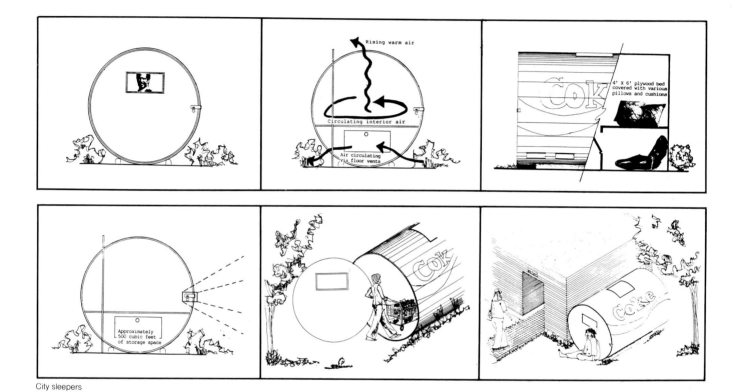

City sleepers

In the summer of 1987 San Francisco architect Donald MacDonald, FAIA, created "city sleepers"—permanent, but moveable, modular units meant to provide clean and dry refuge for some of the architect's indigent neighbors. Made of a plywood box four feet square in section and eight feet long, the prototype units are entered through a side hatch that swings up and can be propped open as a canopy. Inspired by this somewhat controversial project, the Dallas Search for Shelter group, made up of architects and high school students, set about designing their own "city sleepers."

The Skyline High School students' assignment was to design a city sleeper with provisions for "one person, sleeping, entering, viewing, storing, breathing, securing." The sleeper could not exceed eight feet in length, width, or height and had to be made of materials that are readily available, durable, and inexpensive. The total cost was not to exceed $800 per unit. Five students from the school's architecture cluster participated.

Randy Duffy created a triangle of plywood walls and styrofoam insulation, which would be raised off the ground by trailer jacks. It would be secured by locks and have plexiglass windows and a foam-padded bed.

Joe Edman's shelter would closely resemble a single-family house, with sid-

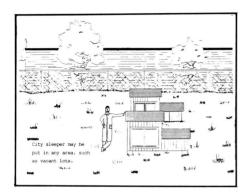

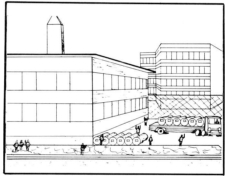

*Opposite page, design by Dustin Slack. This page, clockwise from upper right, designs by Randy Duffy, Gabriel Jairala, Pat Robertson, Joe Edman.*

ing and shingles, although it would be much smaller in size.

Gabriel Jairala would use a 48-inch concrete pipe for the sleeper, which would be well insulated. A plywood board would be placed in the cylinder to make a sleeping space.

Pat Robertson patterned his shelter after a saltbox house. There would be a moveable platform for sleeping and indoor/outdoor carpeting.

Dustin Slack devised a cylindrical, polyethylene shelter. Since the sleeper would resemble an aluminum can, it could become a spot for soft drink and soup advertisements. The revenue gained from the ads could offset the cost of the sleeper.

CONTACT
Robert Welty, AIA
Rawls/Welty, Inc.
Benter Tree Tower #660
16475 Dallas Parkway
Dallas, Tex. 75428
(214)-931-0090

SPONSORS & PARTICIPANTS
Donald MacDonald, FAIA
F&S Partners: Anita Moran, AIA
Rawls Welty & Partners: Robert Welty, AIA
Skyline High School, Architecture Cluster. Students: Randy Duffy, Joe Edman, Gabriel Jairala, Pat Robertson, Dustin Slack. Instructors: Robert N. Batson, AIA, Tom Cox.

# THE CREATION OF SHELTER

MANTRA

My country's name is apathy
My land is smeared with shame
My sightscape moves its homeless hordes
through welfare's turgid flames
The search goes on for rooms and warmth
some closet hooks, a drawer
a hot plate, just for one's own soup—
what liberty is for
Some garments new or even clean
a mirror, a comb, a shelf
a piece of safety, maybe books,
a place to be one's self
some flower pots, taped photographs
a supper shared with friends . . .
are these demands or merely rights?
the road where living bends.

MKW III
(a homeless poet)

# NO PLACE
# TO CALL HOME

Little doubt can exist that the United States is in the midst of a widening housing crisis, as the weakest of its people are relegated to wandering the streets for food and shelter. The plight of the homeless is no longer a rare phenomenon but occurs in city after city, day after day. Although specific causes and remedies are as complex as the homeless themselves, one ingredient is now considered essential for the tragedy to end—an adequate supply throughout the country of stable, affordable housing. Without that housing, the long-term success of rehabilitation efforts seems unlikely.

"The homeless exist on the fringes, taking meals when they find them and shelter where they can. Most have drifted well past the limits of respectability, many deep into alcoholism or mental illness. The public usually views their existence as a shame, a distasteful fact of life met—when it must be faced at all—with averted eyes," *Newsweek* reported on Jan. 2, 1984.

To understand the homeless, one must first dispel the myth that homeless people are on the streets by choice. There is simply no evidence to back up that assertion. If they "choose" to be on the streets, it may be only to avoid the hellish environment found in some shelters—an environment that more closely resembles prisons or asylums.

In the past the homeless were considered bums or drifters—alcoholics, drug addicts, migrant workers (both U.S. citizens and illegal immigrants), and other transients who found cheap housing in flop houses. Now, however, the homeless population more closely resembles in its diversity that of the Great Depression: Today, as then, among the homeless are the young and old, individuals and families, the mentally and physically disabled, and the able-bodied poor. The most dramatic change in the last decade has been a sharp increase in the number of women, children, and families; now families reportedly make up about 30 percent of the overall homeless population. The median age is thought to be 34 years old.

This new underclass of Americans has been described as "retired men on tiny fixed incomes who lost their foothold on self-respect when their single-room cheap hotels closed under pressure of gentrification . . . schizophrenics lost in an outpatient system that would baffle the most dedicated seeker of help . . . unemployed people who have worn out their welcome in overcrowded quarters where families are doubled up . . . young mothers on welfare whose names have been on the eight-year public housing waiting list for only two years . . . old people lost in the anonymous shuffle of big cities, forgotten by whoever once knew them . . . babies who have never slept in a bed or been bathed in a tub."[1]

Recently joining the ranks of the homeless are people suffering from AIDS. "New York Shelters—A Last Stop for Hundreds of AIDS Patients," reads an April 4, 1984, *New York Times* headline. In a city with a significant shortage of long-term public facilities for AIDS patients, many AIDS victims end up "living lives of misery and quiet desperation in the shelters, alone, waiting to die. . . . Suspected AIDS sufferers have been taunted and hounded by other shelter residents." The problem has multiplied significantly since 1984.

Controversy surrounds the exact makeup of the homeless population. "The media and advocates for the homeless portray the homeless population in a false light, particularly families, as people who are simply, suddenly poor. They cannot pay the rent, they cannot find a place to live," according to David Whitman of *U.S. News and World Report.* "Every study of homeless families in urban areas shows that the majority are black or Hispanic, on welfare, and headed by a single mother" and that "homeless families are often deeply troubled long before they lose their apartments."[2]

Precise numbers of homeless persons in this country are difficult to come by: The most often cited estimates range from 250,000 to 4 million persons (as tallied, respectively, by the Department of Housing and Urban Development in 1984 and the Community for Creative Non-Violence, an advocacy group for the homeless located in Washington, D.C., in 1982). The U.S. Conference of Mayors survey of 26 major cities found that during 1987 the demand for emergency shelter increased by an average of 21 percent in all but one of the cities it surveyed. That trend is expected to continue in 1988. No major city has been untouched by the homeless crisis, and it has spread into once unfamiliar territory—the suburbs and rural areas.

*The Washington Post* on June 11, 1987, for example, recounted the plight of the homeless in the suburbs of Washington, D.C., and Baltimore, and beyond: "The governments of these semirural counties in the Washington area are slowly rejecting the notion that homelessness doesn't exist in their communities. They are facing the fact that providing emergency shelter is not just an urban or even suburban problem anymore." On Sept. 8, 1987, the *New York Times* reported similar findings: "The number of homeless people in the suburbs surrounding New York City has doubled in the last three years, officials say, overwhelming emergency services and causing wrenching social change."

In rural areas, the homeless often need to be transported great distances to shelters. In the suburbs individuals and families are transferred from wealthy communities that have few, if any, facilities or services for the homeless to other areas that do. In New York City's suburban Westchester County, the median monthly rent is higher than $700, while the basic state housing grant for a parent and two children is about $285 a month. Federal aid can augment that amount to about $700, but those vouchers are not easy to get. Westchester County reports an estimated 820 homeless families, including about 1,650 children. The Connecticut suburbs of New York City may have as many as 10,000 homeless persons.

A barometer of the seriousness of the homeless problem is the incidence of hunger, since hunger is considered the handmaiden of homelessness. At least 20 million Americans suffer from hunger every month, reports the Harvard Physician

Task Force on Hunger in America. That group also reported that in 1985 malnutrition affected at least 50,000 children in America.

The real issue, however, is not the precise number of the homeless (or the hungry), but the gravity of their situation. The homeless live brutal, debilitating, stressful lives of great hardship. They are subject to violence, weather-related illnesses (pneumonia, frostbite, gangrene, stroke, and heart failure), scabies, tuberculosis and other contagious diseases, alcohol- and drug-related illnesses, and mental anguish. In New York City as many as 50 homeless persons are thought to die on the streets during each of the winter months.

Perhaps the scars of homelessness will later be felt most by the children, who while homeless can often show little interest in school, signs of depression, and a propensity for suicide. "It is not surprising that the children exhibited a wide range of psychological, social, and cognitive problems as well as lags in developmental milestones," suggests psychiatrist Dr. Ellen L. Bassuk, psychologist Lenore Rubin, and mental health consultant Alison S. Lauriat. In shelters in Massachusetts they found a three-month-old boy who was depressed, listless, and unresponsive; a 14-month-old boy who was unable to crawl or to make simple sounds; and a nine-year-old boy who openly talked about killing himself in order to escape the scapegoating and abuse of the other children at the shelter.[3] Often children from homeless shelters aren't welcomed at the local school, the theory being that too many children with potential behavioral or learning problems would be a drain on those teachers. So sometimes the only option is for the children to take buses to the school in the neighborhood they came from, no matter how far away.

The societal causes of homelessness are complex, ranging from the disintegration of the traditional family structure to failures in this country's care of the mentally ill and provision of welfare for the very poor. It is the loss of affordable housing, however, that immediately precipitates homelessness. And, many advocates for the homeless maintain, only when appropriate, affordable housing is secured will the once-homeless respond to the social services they need so badly, such as job training, mental or physical health care, and life skills training.

Finding that low-cost housing, however, is no easy task. (Housing that costs its tenant less than one-third of that person's or family's income is considered low-cost.) Six million American households now spend more than half of their incomes on rent; another 5 million pay more than 35 percent. Between 1972 and 1986, while rents rose, the median incomes of renters dropped from $18,000 to $15,300, according to three reputable sources—the National Housing Task Force, the Harvard/MIT Joint Center for Housing Studies, and the National Low Income Housing Coalition.

According to housing expert Cushing Dolbeare, as of 1987 there were 6 million extremely poor households but only 3 million units that rented for 30 percent, or less, of their incomes. If the trend continues, Cushing suggests, by 1995 there will be 7 million renter households with incomes below $5,000 (in 1983 dollars), but only 2 million units renting at $125 or less.

What is occurring—and what the dramatic rise in homelessness represents—is the most severe housing crisis since the Depression. This crisis may carry well into the 1990s and even beyond. Simply put, more affordable housing is being lost than is being built. The search for shelter has become a Darwinian struggle for housing, in which the weak are losing. And the weakest are falling through society's safety nets onto the street. The 1980s, however, are quite different from the 1930s. Generally, the quality of the housing available today far surpasses that of the 1930s. And whereas the housing woes in the 1930s occurred in a time of tremendous economic upheaval, mass homelessness is occurring today during a period of general economic prosperity.

The practices of both the private and public sectors are suspect. Basically in the 1980s there has been little or no incentive for the private sector to construct affordable housing; meanwhile, construction of federally sponsored housing has trickled to a standstill, and federal subsidizes to owners of existing housing have declined significantly. At the same time hundreds of thousands of affordable units in the private sector have disappeared through arson, abandonment, urban renewal, and gentrification. (Gentrification is the displacement of low- and middle-income people from their houses or apartments, which are then renovated and put back on the market at much higher prices. Only rarely can the poor survive in what becomes a "trendy" neighborhood.) As many as 1 million persons are thought to be displaced every year from private sector housing; many join the ranks of the homeless. The resulting drop in the amount of affordable housing is alarming. The future is foreboding.

Take Saint Paul, for example. Its mayor's office reported to the U.S. Conference of Mayors, "A combination of economic and social problems contribute to homelessness. . . . The housing [persons vulnerable to homelessness are in] is either not affordable, or inadequately sized, or suffers from code deficiencies. These families could live independently and need not be homeless if they had adequate income and housing choices."

Most symbolic of changing development trends is the fate of the flop houses or residential hotels, the traditional stopping point for those seeking temporary and permanent housing at the lowest possible cost. These hotels fell into disdain in the 1960s and became the symbol of urban decay. During the 1970s, they have toppled like bowling pins: By 1982 the nation had lost nearly half its supply, or 1,116,000 units (now called single-room-occupancy units or SROs). Ironically, this housing type is once again considered a viable low-cost alternative, particularly for special groups like single adults, the chronically mentally ill, and the elderly.

In the public sector, President Reagan has led a budget deficit-weary Congress through a near dismantling of the federal low-income housing programs. HUD's budget has dropped from $35.7 billion in fiscal year 1980 to $7 billion in fiscal year 1988. New construction has virtually stopped, with the exception of some housing for the elderly and housing commitments made prior to the Reagan era. The federal government is subsidizing approximately 90,000 new rental units per year, down from 300,000 new units yearly in the peak years of the 1960s and 1970s.

On top of this, the next round of 15-year contracts that the federal government made with private owners of subsidized low-income housing under the Section 236 program will start to expire in the 1990s. Established in the late 1960s, Section 236 offered developers 1 percent mortgage loans, lucrative tax breaks, and in some cases rent subsidies if they provided low-cost housing. But developers were not encouraged to manage and maintain the units adequately. By the early 1970s corruption and defaults were rampant. In 1973 President Nixon put a freeze on all Section 236 housing starts.

In 1974 the Section 8 program was created to replace Section 236; under Section 8 the owners of housing receive a rent subsidy for the difference between the area market rate and the rent the family can afford based on its income. The private commitment was lowered to five years. Upon termination of Section 236 and Section 8 contracts, the private owners are free to convert those units into high-rent condominiums, sell their buildings, or tear them down. The U.S. General Accounting Office predicts a reduction of as many as 900,000 units by 1995 and an additional 800,000 units by the turn of the century.

As the low-income housing market has shrunk, the vacancy rate for the 1.4 million public housing units built over a period of 50 years has tightened to an all-time low—just 3 percent compared with 15 percent two decades ago. In many cities the number of people on waiting lists exceeds the number of units. The waiting time is mind-numbing: 20 years in Miami, 18 years in New York City, four years in Savannah, Ga.; some cities have simply stopped taking applicants. The country is actually losing public housing; some 70,000 public housing units are being abandoned yearly, according to HUD estimates. The remaining public housing stock is in desperate need of repairs—as much as $21.5 billion worth, according to HUD.

The Reagan Administration has proposed selling public housing to tenants. Critics contend that these people are least able to purchase and maintain the housing. Critics also argue that the Reagan Administration's turn toward housing allowance vouchers to renters does not guarantee the availability of low-cost units and, therefore, does nothing for the "supply side." In many places low-cost housing is already near impossible to find.

When sizing up the financial commitment this country makes to housing low-income households, what must not be overlooked, advocates for the homeless and for low-income households assert, is the massive aid to middle- and upper-income homeowners that the federal government gives in the form of mortgage tax credits. In 1987 those tax credits totaled $44 billion a year, about three times what the federal government spends directly on housing aid to lower-income households.

Besides the decline of affordable housing, the generally cited causes of homelessness are unemployment and underemployment, cuts in public welfare assistance, drug and alcohol abuse, mental illness and lack of services needed by the mentally ill, and personal crises ranging from household breakups to domestic violence to health problems.

Particularly vulnerable to homelessness are people who are chronically mentally ill. Theirs is a tragic story. Until the mid-1950s, a large percentage of the mentally ill found complete care in state hospitals; often patients with severe illnesses found long-term refuge there. The discovery of antipsychotic drugs led to the release of patients on the theory that these new medications could control symptoms of the mental illnesses and that it was more humane for the chronically mentally ill to return to their communities. There they could obtain outpatient care at community mental health centers. In the first wave, approximately 200,000 patients were released.

The 1960s brought continued public outcries over the deplorable conditions at state hospitals—perhaps most starkly characterized by Tom Keasy's popular novel and film, *One Flew Over the Cuckoo's Nest.* Hundreds of thousands more patients were released. By 1985 there were fewer than 150,000 psychiatric patients in hospitals nationwide, compared to 550,000 in 1955. The chronically mentally ill were left to fend for themselves, as few of the community support centers materialized. The 1963 goal of starting 2,000 community mental-health centers nationwide was 1,300 short by 1980. "The concept of moving comprehensive treatment and care from the institution to community auspices was basically a good one. . . . But the implementation was terribly flawed," the American Psychiatric Association's task force on the homeless concluded in 1984.

For the chronically mentally ill, maintaining a decent paying, full-time, or even part-time, job can be difficult. Consequently they can lose their lodgings, if they are living independently. Or they can fail to take proper care of themselves and once again suffer the damaging consequences of their illness. The most unfortunate lose any permanent connection with society. "It's a merry-go-round," said one 48-year-old schizophrenic in New York City. "You go to the hospital, then they dump you into those Dante Inferno shelters and then you go back again. This system doesn't make a man go up. It makes him go down."[4]

Again, it is difficult to offer a precise count of homeless persons who are mentally ill; experts say 20 to 50 percent of the homeless population, maybe

substantially more. As Dr. Irene Levine of the National Institute of Mental Health suggests: "The very state of homelessness can cause varying degrees of mental illness in relatively short periods of time."

Job displacement can cause homelessness, particularly in the case of industrial workers whose skills are no longer useful in the new, high-tech society. "During the decade of the 1970s, at least 38 million jobs in basic industry were permanently lost," says Dr. Richard Ropers of UCLA's Developmental Disabilities Immersions Program and co-director of Los Angeles's Basic Shelter and Research Project. New York City lost 80,000 blue collar jobs between 1980 and 1985. Many workers in obvious need of retraining are able to find only low-paying service jobs. So even if working, they are susceptible to homelessness. The U.S. Conference of Mayors found in 1987 that 22 percent of the homeless in the 26 cities it surveyed had full- or part-time jobs—another disturbing trend.

Take the conditions in Louisville as reported to the U.S. Conference of Mayors. "In our city a family of three needs at least $7 per hour to meet their basic needs. Many of the working poor make considerably less." In San Francisco, "high and constantly rising costs of rent, food, shelter, and clothing have reached a level far in excess of the income of the working poor. The working poor are constantly losing ground in their battle to survive—this often leads to a deterioration of their mental health and family interactions."

The lack or inadequacy of public benefits can also push an individual or a family into homelessness. The mayor's office in Norfolk, Va., reports, "The presence of family income spent on shelter is constantly increasing, leaving very little money to meet other needs. The new poor have been rejected for public assistance because of strict regulations. They have gone to the streets or shelters, or have become names on waiting lists."

Once homeless, families are often split up, with the child or children placed in the homes of friends or members of the extended family. The children may be turned over for foster care while their parents seek emergency, and then more permanent, housing. Adequate day care is difficult to find, a situation that obviously hurts mothers seeking full-time employment. Under these circumstances homeless families often choose instead to live in their cars, move from campground to campground, or find refuge in abandoned houses.

Homeless youths aged 18 to 20 have a hard time finding help: They are too old for traditional foster care but too young to benefit from services provided in shelters for adults. That age group is particularly vulnerable to the streets—and prostitution and drugs. Often they live in abandoned houses, which they call "squats" or "empties."

"Frequently street youths band together and sleep in abandoned buildings downtown," says Virginia Price, clinical director at Bridge over Troubled Waters, a private agency in Boston that assists homeless youths. "They tend to be secretive even among themselves about the location of the 'empties.' As more youth find out about a new 'empty' they must be included, since anyone denied admission might disclose the building to the authorities. As more youths join the band, so does the incidence of violence. Most of these youths have grown up in families where violence is routinely used to handle interpersonal conflict," she continued.[5]

For victims of domestic violence—battered women and their children—the situation is bleak. Sometimes the only safe and affordable refuge is a women's shelter, which, because of demand, may restrict the length of an individual's stay. When that time limit is reached, the women and their children may have no option but to return to intolerable family situations.

How long a person is homeless varies significantly. Dr. Michael Vergare and Dr. Anthony Arce, psychiatrists with the Albert Einstein Medical Center in Philadelphia, have suggested three groupings: (1) the chronic, who are homeless for more than 30 continuous days although many, if not most, have been homeless for months or years; (2) the episodic, who tend to alternate for varying periods of time between being domiciled and being homeless, with homelessness usually lasting less than 30 days; and (3) the situational, for whom homelessness is the temporary result of an acute life crisis.

Once the threshold of homelessness has been crossed, the nightmarish quest becomes universal: Where to find a safe haven for the night and a secure home for the future. Theoretically, housing for the homeless is a three-tier system of emergency, transitional, and long-term shelter. A person or family should move through the system as quickly as possible. But more often than not, that process is slowed by high demand and short supply.

Ideally, emergency shelter will be provided for a few days to a few weeks. During that time the longer-term needs of each individual should be identified, such as income support, job training, mental health services, and permanent housing. The largest shelters usually are the public ones; most simply offer a temporary respite from inclement weather and the dangers of the street. There is no sense of permanency or privacy; bathroom and storage facilities are inadequate; and there are few supportive services. The facilities are often run-down and the buildings exceedingly unattractive. Conditions can be in gross violation of building codes. Some suggest that emergency shelters can adequately handle 300 or 350 persons, a figure that others maintain is much too high.

Perhaps one of the most notorious shelters in the country is the Fort Washington emergency shelter in New York City. Of that shelter Ellen Baxter and Kim Hopper wrote for the Community Service Society in New York City: "The frightening scale and Dickensian conditions of public emergency shelter effectively exclude those most in need of a protective setting." Located in an armory in upper Manhattan, Baxter and Hopper described it as a shelter "where chaos prevailed . . . 900 men slept on iron cots set in rows on a single drill floor, with the hallucinations and bizarre behaviors of the mentally disturbed among them hardly quelled by the seven to 12 staff members on a shift."[6]

The cleaner, smaller, better-run, and safer private shelters generally administered by nonprofit or church groups (some with local, state, or federal funds) strive to offer a sense of caring, respect, and dignity to their guests. Capacities range from five to 300 beds. But often there is little privacy, little space to share belongings, few opportunities to establish connections in a social atmosphere that could change at any time. Funding can be provided by local, state, or federal governments, or private organizations.

Transitional housing is designed to suit individual needs as much as possible. Ideally provided for three to six months, such housing can take the form of apartments, shared facilities, duplexes for families, or single-family houses. In addition to the traditional apartments or single-family houses, shared facilities—particularly SROs and group homes—are seen as legitimate long-term housing.

Advocates of the homeless suggest, however, that homelessness is a complex, multidimensional problem that cannot be addressed by providing shelter alone. "Many localities have unfortunately opted either to do nothing or to provide only emergency shelters," suggest Jon Erickson and Charles Wilhelm in *Housing the Homeless*. "The short-term emergency shelter may appear to be the cheapest solution, but unless the cycle of homelessness is broken, the need for more shelters can only grow. To break the cycle of homelessness through the development of comprehensive and coordinated programs may in fact be less expensive in the long run."[7]

As the number of homeless persons began to multiply rapidly in the early 1980s and continues today, the providers of housing and services have not been able to keep up with the demand. The U.S. Conference of Mayors found in its 1987 survey of 26 cities that 23 percent of the demand for emergency shelter in those cities goes unmet. Seattle reports that "there is a lack of space and resources to meet the critical demand for emergency shelter." New Orleans reports "if possible, no one is turned away, but the available shelters are generally packed to capacity." Once in an emergency shelter, it may be hard for a person to "move up" into transitional or permanent shelter because the demand outstrips capacity. If the emergency shelter has a time limit on a person's stay, that person may, once again, wind up on the street. If not, the emergency shelter, by default, may become more permanent housing.

More significantly, advocates for the homeless have grave concerns that in the long run well-intended efforts to shelter the homeless, especially on an emergency basis, will become less rather than more humane. Both a shelter's services and design are suspect, particularly if the shelter becomes an end rather than a means to an end. "While emergency shelters are essential in order to provide the homeless with food, clothing, and shelter, they are only stop-gap measures and must not be viewed as permanent solutions," suggest Dr. Frank R. Lipton and Dr. Albert Sabatini, psychiatrists with Bellevue Psychiatric Hospital, New York City. "The overcrowding, oppressiveness, and squalid conditions existing in many shelters, emergency or otherwise, are as unacceptable as the conditions that once existed in state hospitals. Present-day shelters are reminiscent of the almshouses or poorhouses of colonial America that were used to 'care for' the aged, the destitute, the criminals, the deranged, and other socially undesirable groups."[8]

Designers of shelters and providers of shelter services must walk a fine line between providing decent, short-term housing that is so desperately needed and having that emergency and transitional housing become inappropriate long-term shelter for hundreds or thousands. Regardless of type, the shelter design and services must respect the dignity of each individual—that person's basic human right to decent shelter, food, education, employment, and medical care.

Meanwhile, the number of the less visible victims of the housing crisis also continues to increase. Nicknamed "couch people," these homeless people—lacking the resources to afford housing on their own (even with federal and state aid)—tend to drift from place to place, doubling or tripling up with friends or relatives. These alliances, if necessary for extended periods of time, are often uneasy. Recent estimates by advocates for the homeless put the number of "couch" families in New York City at 100,000, including up to 200,000 children.

New York City's is not an isolated experience. Seattle's Mayor Charles Royer noted in May 1985, "For every homeless person in Seattle, there are 10 others who are at risk and who need some

kind of assistance." In fact, the estimated 250,000 to 4 million homeless persons nationwide are thought to represent only the tip of a much larger iceberg. Besides those doubling or tripling up, many people live in substandard, decrepit buildings or are barely able to afford their monthly rent and monthly fear eviction.

The housing crisis no longer affects only this country's poorest. Homeownership among the middle class is declining, for the first time since World War II. For more and more people, the only option is to "trickle down" rather than "trickle up." Robert Hayes, founder of the National Coalition for the Homeless, calls it "a Darwinian struggle for housing. And the weak are losing." It isn't just the stereotypical "bums" or the poorest of the poor; the crisis has reached some working people and families, even those once considered safely positioned in the middle class.

Means of providing decent emergency and transitional shelter for the homeless and long-term, low-cost housing must be found; solutions will not come easily. Reaching the goal of decent housing for every American—as first decreed by Congress in 1949—will require the efforts of a broad range of players from both the public and private sectors. Only then can Americans be assured that by the turn of the century the suffering caused by the affordable housing crisis will not run deeper.

# PARTNERSHIPS FOR HOUSING

As the housing crisis has expanded during the past decade, so have efforts to mitigate the suffering. Throughout the country advocates for the homeless have campaigned for the right to decent shelter for all Americans, courts have ruled in favor of zoning laws that require a mixture of people with varying incomes in neighborhoods once closed to the poor, and state and local governments, nonprofit organizations, and private sector leaders have devised creative methods of raising money to build and maintain shelters for the homeless and low-cost housing. And although most housing experts argue that the federal government's active participation in providing low-cost housing remains crucial, they concede that the days of substantial subsidies and massive new federal housing programs most likely are over. As a consequence community-based partnerships between the public and private sectors are growing more and more popular and important.

In the early 1980s homelessness was viewed as a short-term housing problem in which the provision of shelter and food on an emergency basis was the main objective. But as the decade progressed, so has the understanding of how closely the rise in homelessness is linked to a decreasing supply of low-cost housing in this country. Now, any discussion of housing the homeless would be remiss if an examination of low-cost housing was not included. Advocates for the homeless have begun fighting for what they consider a basic right in this country — the right to decent, affordable, permanent shelter.

The right to shelter was articulated by a homeless man in Phoenix to Louisa Stark, a former president of the National Coalition for the Homeless. "We're not all winos and we're not all crazies," the man said. "We have some needs. One of our needs is a job, one of our needs is clothing, one is food, but the most important need is a place to be and continue to be."[1]

A leader in the right-to-shelter campaign is the National Coalition's founder, Robert Hayes. As a young lawyer working for a prestigious Wall Street law firm, he became outraged about the condition of the homeless people he passed daily on his way to work. Hayes gradually learned that those men and women found the streets and subways "less dangerous and degrading," in their words, than the city's public shelters. Hayes concluded that the "demand for shelter beds was far lower than the true need since conditions at the municipal shelters effectively deterred many of the homeless from seeking shelter."

In October 1979 in the case *Callahan v. Carey*, Hayes filed suit against the city and state of New York on behalf of six homeless men. The state and local governments were charged with not living up to their constitutional responsibilities to provide shelter for these homeless men based on provisions in New York's state constitution, the state's Social Service Law, the city's municipal law, and the equal protection provision of the U.S. Constitution. In December 1979 the court granted the plaintiffs a preliminary injunction that required the city to provide shelter to them and anyone who requested it. During the summer of 1980 the city agreed to supply all applicants with shelter of a quality to be mandated by the courts. It did not, however, grant the plaintiffs' request that shelters be community based, fearing insurmountable opposition from those communities.

Within three years the number of emergency beds available to homeless men and women in New York City jumped from 1,000 to 4,000, hardly a total victory. "The court became an independent means of catalyzing broad-based popular support for reform. For this reason, litigation as an advocacy tool should be viewed within the context of an overall strategy for social change," suggest Kim Hopper and L. Stuart Cox, advocates for the homeless in New York City. "The crucial transformation appears to be the reversal of what had been, to date, commonly accepted as fair policy that the claim of the homeless poor on public resources had no legitimacy other than that gratuitously extended by officials of the state. What was popularly and officially perceived as a plea became, through the

101

agency of the court, endowed with the dignity and power of a right."[2]

Since that landmark case, the right to shelter has been won by single women, the chronically mentally ill, and families. The practice of local, state, and federal governments to deny welfare payments to people with no fixed address (including those living in shelters for the homeless) has been successfully challenged in the courts. In other cases, lawyers have argued that shelter is an essential element of treatment for thousands of people released from state mental hospitals. In addition the right of homeless people to vote and to be eligible for food stamps and medical assistance has been challenged.

"Without question, litigation has proved to be an effective means of securing emergency relief. But with thousands upon thousands of destitute city dwellers without homes, mass provision of minimally humane asylum for the homeless poor is but part of the solution—a necessary, palliative first-step," Hopper and Cox maintain. The ultimate goal is the availability of adequate low-cost, permanent housing.

An approach to guaranteeing shelter used less often is through public referendum. The first right to shelter referendum passed by a substantial margin in the District of Columbia in November 1984. Other similar referendums guaranteeing overnight shelter to anyone in need have been passed in Philadelphia and New York City. This approach is highly controversial. Critics charge that the homeless will flock to these cities and, consequently, rapidly diminish these cities' resources. Proponents find the provision of housing limited in scope; an array of social services are needed too, they argue. As Mary Orton, executive director of Central Arizona Shelter Services, noted, "We've learned you don't do anybody a favor by offering [the homeless] three hots and a cot—hot meals and a free place to live."

Some, however, fear the pendulum could swing too far the other way. New York City's Mayor Ed Koch announced in February 1988 a controversial plan to involuntarily commit the sickest of the street people to psychiatric institutions. Initially fewer than 100 homeless persons were rounded up. The first patient to be detained, Joyce Brown, successfully contested her commitment in the courts, even though she was obviously suffering from severe schizophrenia.

Meanwhile, with the same intensity as the right-to-shelter advocates, many who live in residential neighborhoods are banning together to keep shelters and low-cost housing out. The phenomenon is called NIMBY—"not in my backyard." These residents may approve in theory the development of housing for homeless or low-income people. In fact, *U.S. News and World Report* cited in its Feb. 29, 1988, issue a recent national poll showing that "the country's voters rank homelessness and hunger as the second most important issue facing the next President—just behind reducing the federal deficit." Yet, when that housing is to be placed in one's own neighborhood, the cry often becomes "not in my backyard." It is estimated that for every group residence built for the chronically mentally ill, three others are blocked, even though evidence shows that such facilities, if dispersed throughout a community, generally do not decrease property values in the neighborhood.

What often happens in a given city, then, is that shelters for the homeless and low-income housing tend to be developed in the same neighborhoods. There the complaint is, "We're becoming a dumping ground" for such facilities, a sentiment that unfortunately is often correct. Obviously one of the big attractions of the "dumping ground" is the low property rates. So, the objective today is to obtain property for shelters and low-income housing at lower than market rates in the less saturated neighborhoods.

Another NIMBY cry is that introducing shelters or low-cost housing into a community will increase crime. "Shelters in which inadequate supervision is

provided can be ominous neighbors. Large municipal shelters usually have poor staff-to-client ratios as
well as unstructured programs. Residents of these
shelters are faced with many idle hours, and they
are perceived in the community as intimidating
figures," conclude Rose Anello and Tillie Shuster,
authors of *Community Relations Strategies: A Handbook
for Sponsors of Community-Based Programs for the Homeless*.
But this outcome is not universal. "Programs that
employ adequate management can enhance the
safety of a community," Anello and Shuster continue.

Anello and Shuster devised for the Community
Service Society of New York City a strategy for
winning community acceptance of housing for the
homeless. That strategy revolves around this theory:
"Sound planning, adequate program development,
and constant and early contact with the host
community are all important in overcoming obstacles," they suggest. Their recommendations include
the following, among others:
• Develop a community relations campaign as early
as possible. It is better to allow the community an
opportunity to assist in site selection rather than
present them with a packaged proposal. However,
be clear about what you want to do.
• Research local codes for restrictions on building
and population types. Also remember to budget
extra time in the development process if you need
to work through the local planning commission to
acquire city-owned property.
• Do not call needless attention to your project.
The words *homeless* and *shelters* can alarm many
communities. Phrases such as *residence, housing, congre-
gate facility* can convey the same message without the
negative connotations.
• Keep supporters informed of your progress, both
the problems and the successes.
• Select a site and community appropriate for the
population you intend to serve. A building without
an elevator may not be appropriate for the elderly.
Selecting a site for young adults or the mentally ill
near a child-care center or school may mobilize
community opposition.

• Have one staff person in charge of the development process.
• As much as possible, give priority to local homeless populations.
• If you are selecting a site in a community you do
not serve, assess whether your program could be
cosponsored by a local community-based organization.
• Always assess and be aware of legal and regulatory
requirements.[3]

The most widely used tool for keeping certain
populations out of a neighborhood is exclusionary
zoning. This can take the form of zoning ordinance
provisions, such as large lot requirements, minimum
unit area requirements, maximum numbers of unrelated tenants, and prohibitions on certain types of
housing (for example, garden apartments or group
homes). Exclusionary zoning has been used widely
since the 1950s, and particularly by the nation's
more exclusive suburban communities, primarily to
keep out public housing projects.

In the 1949 Housing Act the U.S. Congress
pledged "a decent home and suitable living
environment for every American family." In
1969 that pledge was renewed by the nation's lawmakers as a strong protest against the housing
segregation that existed between decaying urban
neighborhoods and exclusive, wealthy suburbs.
But, housing and urban development policies of the
1970s did little to improve the situation. "During
the last 15 years, there have been hundreds, if not
thousands, of efforts by community organizations,
housing sponsors, and developers to foster integration through the use of federal housing programs,"
says housing and land development expert Alan
Mallach. "But only a small fraction were successful
in the limited sense of bringing a group of housing
units into being, often only as a result of litigation
or of enormous effort expanded over a considerable
number of years."[4] Those practices are being challenged in the courts today.

A landmark challenge to exclusionary zoning —
widely known as *Mount Laurel II*—came in 1983

when the New Jersey Supreme Court ruled that adoption of an inclusionary housing program would be expected, if not explicitly required, of any municipality that did not meet its obligation to provide its fair share of regional low- and moderate-income housing needs. In the 1975 case *Southern Burlington County NAACP et al. v. Township of Mount Laurel* (commonly known as *Mount Laurel I*) the court had decreed that each municipality in New Jersey must provide a "realistic opportunity" through land-use controls to provide for its fair share of regional housing. The 1983 *Mount Laurel II* ruling established an exact municipal obligation toward reaching that goal.

In *Mount Laurel II* the court established two practical conditions to govern such inclusionary programs: first, a municipality should require that units be developed for low-income tenants even where housing subsidies were not available; and, second, dwelling units were to remain affordable to lower-income households over an extended length of time, although no precise time period was established. A recent attempt to force application of *Mount Laurel II* provisions in New York City courts failed.

Broadly speaking, inclusionary zoning is the reverse of exclusionary zoning: The goal of inclusionary zoning is to foster the development of affordable housing as an integral part of other residential development. Generally, a percentage of the units are to be allotted for households with low incomes, often defined as a percentage of the median income of the area. Some localities provide incentives to developers, such as density bonuses, modifications of the normal development requirements, and use of federal funding to lower project costs.

Now inclusionary zoning is considered by some to "hold the great promise of becoming the most significant means by which housing opportunities for lower-income households, in a racially and economically integrated environment, can and will be provided in the United States in the coming

years," in planner Alan Mallach's words.[5] It may also be the only effective way that the private sector can be encouraged to develop low-cost housing.

In the early 1980s Mallach documented 72 mandatory or voluntary inclusionary housing programs at the state and local levels. Most of those local programs are modest in size, with a few exceptions, such as Montgomery County, Md. That municipality offers density bonuses to encourage the development of affordable housing projects. In addition, one-eighth of the units in new residential developments are to be set aside for moderate-income families.

Thirty-eight of the 72 programs Mallach found were in California. The preamble of the model inclusionary zoning ordinance written by the California Department of Housing and Community Development reads: "The housing shortage for persons of low- and moderate-income is detrimental to the public health, safety, and welfare, since low- and moderate-income households are forced to live in unsafe, unsanitary, overcrowded housing, and/or housing that they cannot afford. Thus, in the name of the public interest, inclusionary programs promote the development of community housing that would not otherwise be built."[6]

A technique to generate low-cost housing from nonresidential, urban development is called linkage. One of the most highly regarded efforts is San Francisco's office and housing production program, which is based on the theory that "large-scale office developments in the city and county have attracted and continue to attract additional employees to the city, and there is a causal connection between such developments and the need for additional housing in the city, particularly housing affordable to households of low and moderate income."[7]

Under this mandatory ordinance developers of new office buildings in San Francisco have three options: (1) construction of housing or participation in a joint venture to construct housing, at the rate of 0.386 units of new housing for every 1,000 square feet of office development; (2) payment of a of $5.34 for each square foot of new office space in lieu of not constructing housing; or (3) a combination of the two. Recently the San Francisco ordinance was modified to allow money to go toward the development of child-care facilities, transit improvements, and the arts. Through a similar program in Boston, all large-scale commercial developments are subject to the city's mandatory linkage program—retail businesses, office buildings, and institutional, educational, and hotel projects.

Linkage can also be voluntary. In Seattle and Miami, for instance, developers can receive increased floor-to-area ratios (FAR) if they make a cash contribution to a housing fund or build low-cost housing. In Jersey City, N.J., Cambridge, Mass., Chicago, and Washington, D.C., developers of large downtown commercial buildings can receive on a case-by-case basis generous density bonuses if they build housing or contribute to the housing fund.

As of early 1988 a total of 16 states and 12 cities had established housing trust funds that could be used for the development of shelters for the homeless or low-cost housing. Revenues come from a variety of sources: taxes on off-shore oil leases (California); real estate transfer taxes (Maine and Florida); a housing finance agency's excess reserve funds (Kentucky and Maine); and specially marked state and city appropriations (New York). In Cherry Hill, N.J., impact fees (1.5 percent of the median price of new construction in the region) are placed on new market-rate housing. In New Hampshire corporations, individuals, banks, church groups, and other organizations contribute to a community housing loan fund.

Although inclusionary zoning may prove to be a valuable tool in generating low-cost housing, the future prospects of linkage may be dimmer. If the office boom that begun in the mid-1970s gives way to slower downtown development, which seems to be the trend, then the chances for successful linkage diminish. Increased densities achieved through municipal bonuses are not always viewed favorably from the standpoint of quality of living. Legal questions

may also arise. In 1987 the California Supreme Court ruled in *Nollan v. California Coastal Commission* that if state and local governments place conditions on development approvals that are not directly related to the objectives of the regulations or problems created by the development, the result may be a taking of property for which the government must compensate the landowner. If this case stands, obviously the original incentive for linkage is lost. And new limitations placed on real estate development through tax reform may work against linkage.

Since the mid-1950s federal tax code provisions have encouraged development of rental housing, and in the 1970s developers of low-cost housing were given additional tax incentives. Typically these have taken the form of accelerated depreciation and lower rates on capital gains. Lenders' bad debts were treated favorably in terms of taxes, as were construction financing and other development costs.

These and other tax provisions were substantially altered by the Tax Reform Act of 1986. "In addition to the obstacles to producing housing for the poor, the new tax law also makes it more difficult to maintain low- and moderate-income benefits as existing housing turns over, regardless of its subsidy stature. Lower marginal tax rates and the elimination of capital gains rates, among other provisions, remove additional incentives based on tax avoidance," Phillip L. Clay, of the Massachusetts Institute of Technology, suggests in an analysis of low-income rental housing for the Neighborhood Reinvestment Corporation. Damaging to the supply of low-cost rental housing, Clay maintains, are the following provisions:
• the reduction of the value of deductibility of interest and real estate tax expenses;
• the increase in the depreciation period from as few as 15 years to 27.5 years;
• the repeal of capital gain preferences, which eliminates any difference between taxes paid on

ordinary income and taxes paid on capital gains;
• the further restriction of states' ability to issue tax-exempt bonds, which in recent years have provided financing at below-market interest rates;
• the substantial reduction of the ability of limited partners to invest in real estate to obtain loses that help reduce tax liabilities resulting from other income;
• the elimination of the value of tax syndication, which often generated cash (for profits or subsidy) valued at 20 to 25 percent of the total mortgage amount.[8]

The effects of the Tax Reform Act of 1986 will be far-reaching. "Tax reform," Clay maintains, "provides a definite disincentive to the purchase or rehabilitation of any property for low-income use without an adequate and long-term subsidy tied to the housing. The fact that some tenants have certificates is not sufficient since cash assistance is portable and, therefore, is not a reliable stream of income on which to base a loan." Others believe that the tax changes will favor more rehabilitation over new construction and will elevate the role of nonprofit and community-based housing groups in housing production.

An early indication of possible responses to tax reform come from New York City. There, the *New York Times* reported on Oct. 11, 1988, a nonprofit group overseeing the creation of 1,000 apartments for low-income families raised more than 30 percent of the project's total cost—or $25 million— from corporate investors. According to a spokesman of the Local Initiatives Support Corporation (LISC), ten percent of these new units will be reserved for homeless families. Under the LISC plan, the participating corporations will each earn tax credits equal to a return of 157 percent of their investment over 190 years. In partnership with the city and LISC will be 13 corporations, the largest among them the Continental Insurance Co., American Express, Dime Savings Bank, New York Life Insurance Co., and Pfizer Inc.

It is too early to tell if such projects will be repeated elsewhere in this magnitude. So, in the meantime, federal tax reforms must be countered by changes in local and state policies, maintain Michael A. Stegman and J. David Holden in *Nonfederal Housing Programs: How States and Localities Are Responding to Federal Cutbacks in Low-Income Housing.* "Despite the limiting effects of tax reform, for sustained levels of low-income housing production to be achieved, the continued availability of tax-exempt financing must be assured—and supplemented by state and local subsidies, in order to lower development costs and drive down interest rates below their tax-exempt levels. If it turns out that the restrictions of the Tax Reform Act prove to be so intractable that higher-cost taxable bonds must substitute for tax-exempt financing, the resulting higher debt service requirements will call for even more generous subsidies to make low-income projects feasible."[9]

One of the most successful tax-exempt financing programs is Massachusetts's State Housing Assistance for Rental Production (SHARP) program, a shallow-subsidy loan program calling for at least 25 percent of units of privately sponsored multifamily housing to be occupied by households with incomes below 80 percent of the areawide median.

SHARP is just one example of the swelling response by state and local governments to the federal government's withdrawal from its traditional housing programs. In fact, the 1980s has witnessed a tremendous blossoming of public and private, as well as local and national, groups working together to provide decent low-cost housing:
• Greater Miami Neighborhoods is providing development services to six neighborhood and citywide low-income housing groups. Since 1985 it has raised more than $1.5 million from local government and the business community for loans, grants, and operating expenses, producing initial commitments for 266 dwelling units.
• Headquartered in Sacramento, Calif., and operating in 10 western states, the Rural Community

Assistance Corporation has helped local communities develop 20,000 units of housing, including 5,000 constructed using self-help techniques. The organization operates on grants and contracts from government agencies.

• In Baltimore The Loading Dock, Inc., a nonprofit salvage operation, collects donated new and used building materials for sale to low-income housing groups and nonprofit organizations at one-third the retail price. Donors receive tax write-offs.

• In Tennessee the Chattanooga Neighborhood Enterprise, an alliance of city government and private lenders, has embraced a plan to make low-income housing in the city—some 14,000 units—fit and affordable within 10 years.

• A cosponsor of the Search for Shelter program, Neighborhood Reinvestment Corporation is the umbrella organization of the Neighborhood Housing Services, which are located in 137 cities. The network also includes the Apartment Improvement Program and the Mutual Housing Association. Results to date include the rehabilitation of 58,000 units of affordable housing and construction of another 586 units on formerly vacant lots. Almost 3,000 tenants have received financial support enabling them to purchase their homes.

• The Cleveland Housing Network, an umbrella corporation of nonprofit housing development corporations, acquires and rehabilitates vacant and abandoned houses for sale to low-income families. By the end of 1986, CHN had renovated 450 housing units.

• Founded in 1988, the Massachusetts Housing Partnership consists of state agencies giving local housing partnerships financial and technical support. Efforts are geared toward four goals: (1) to increase the supply of affordable housing; (2) to identify local urban resources—vacant lots and buildings, properties whose taxes have not been paid and property owners holding dilapidated structures or vacant land; (3) to encourage local governments to combine growth management and affordable housing initiatives; and (4) to encourage the devel-

© Shephard Sherbell, Picture Group

opment of housing for persons with special needs.

• The Chicago South Shore Bank linked deposit program supports neighborhood housing and community development. Basically, individuals, government agencies, corporations, and foundations invest funds in a bank at low or no interest based on the bank's commitment to in turn use the money in community developments.

• The state of California has six housing programs for low- and very-low income persons: the rental housing construction program, the emergency shelter program, the special user housing rehabilitation program, the California self-help housing program, the farm labor housing rehabilitation program, and the senior citizens shared housing program.

• In 1987 the Housing Authority of the City of Houston initiated three programs in reaction to hard economic times there. First, the authority purchased 207 suburban houses repossessed by the Federal Housing Administration to add to the city's stock of public housing. Second, the housing authority requested that the Houston Apartment Association make 200 privately-owned apartment units available to low-income Houstonians who are on the public housing waiting list and have demonstrated quality living skills. And, third, the housing authority purchased a vacant Holiday Inn to convert it into 205 subsidized apartments for elderly and handicapped residents.

• In Mississippi the Delta Housing Development Corporation has supervised the construction of 125 self-help housing units and has constructed 157 others. Another 50 have been rehabilitated and 2,000 units weatherized.

This list merely touches the surface. In the second volume of *New Money and New Methods: A Catalog of State and Local Initiatives in Housing and Community Development*, Mary K. Nenno and George S. Colyer state that "the task of identifying the important initiatives in housing and community development currently underway at state and local levels is an awesome one.... It is clear to us that the scope and depth of the initiatives represent more than a passing phenomenon. We believe that larger, independent roles in housing and community development at state and local levels are here to stay."

So much activity is occurring at the state and local levels and in the private and public sectors that only a cursory acknowledgment can be given here. In their survey for the Urban Land Institute, Stegman and Holden found "a rich variety of activities.... To a greater extent than ever before, housing needs are being recognized as a legitimate area of state and local concern."[10] While states and localities are providing more public funds for housing from their general coffers, there is also an aggressive search for new revenue sources, including new real estate taxes, fees on new development, the use of excess monies from finance agencies and other bond reserves, and community funds.

Some examples: Alaska, Louisiana, and Memphis have pioneered the use of taxable housing bonds as a financing technique. Atlantic City has imposed a 2 percent tax on gross casino revenues; Montgomery County, Md., has imposed a 4 percent tax on the initial sale of rental buildings being converted into condominiums.

The formation of partnerships—among nonprofit, corporate, financial, public, and community players, and others—to produce housing is proliferating. In fact, Stegman and Holden see these partnerships

as the "most significant and potentially far-reaching low-income housing innovation at the local level."

Some private corporations have even set up nonprofit organizations to channel profits from their private sector activities to local housing, community development, and economic development ventures. The best known are the Enterprise Foundation and LISC. Both groups work with community based organizations to reduce the cost of rehabilitating and building low-cost housing and to lower the cost of financing. The centerpiece of each program is technical assistance in designing, funding, and operating housing.

LISC was created in 1979 by the Ford Foundation in cooperation with major insurance and banking companies to "assist local nonprofit organizations to draw new public and private resources into their efforts to revitalize communities and neighborhoods." It has provided financial and technical aid to 500 community development corporations for housing—including construction and rehabilitation of 14,000 units—and other physical and economic development projects.

Founded in 1981, the Enterprise Foundation's financial backing comes mainly from the profits of Columbia, Md., developer James Rouse's festival marketplaces. The Enterprise Foundation network includes 70 nonprofit groups in 27 cities. Its goal is "to help the poor help themselves to decent, livable housing, and out of poverty and dependence into self-sufficiency."

Some partnerships are created to complete successfully one community-based project. In New York City in 1986, for instance, Chemical Bank committed $510,000 to assist community groups through recoverable grant programs and for general operating support. The recoverable grants finance feasibility-study costs associated with projects that focus on the rehabilitation of city-owned buildings that are foreclosed or whose future is uncertain. Community-based grantees who successfully complete their projects repay the feasibility-study grants without interest. For the projects that are never realized, no repayment is required.

Other partnerships have more ambitious agendas. The Boston Housing Partnership and the Chicago Housing Partnership, for instance, coordinate the delivery of a high volume of low-cost housing units. These organizations have three main functions, Stegman and Holden suggest: (1) to organize and manage complex programs that can salvage declining and abandoned housing and convert it into decent, affordable housing for low- and moderate-income families; (2) to mobilize funding and other resources of the community and government agencies for neighborhood-based organizations, so that the public and private sectors can attack housing problems jointly; and (3) to provide technical assistance to community-based sponsors of low- and moderate-income housing for the purpose of enhancing their capacities to develop and manage housing. It is interesting to note that both partnerships were formed on the recommendation of blue-ribbon panels that included major business interests.

Also far-reaching in its goals is the BRIDGE Housing Corporation, a nonprofit organization established in 1983 that produces low-cost housing by itself or in conjunction with neighborhood-based organizations in the nine-county San Francisco Bay area. BRIDGE president Don Turner says that the organization's aim is to "provide housing in some volume, not just in token numbers." Specifically, the aim is to supply 5 percent of the area's multifamily housing, which equals about 1,000 to 1,500 units per year. The majority of the below-market units produced each year are mixed in with market-rate housing, with no design distinctions between them. And BRIDGE stresses excellence in site planning and design. "Every project has to be a showcase. You have to serve the consumer, but, just as importantly, you have to satisfy the nearby neighbors," Turner adds.

BRIDGE plays five different roles: (1) private developer; (2) sole developer invited to use city-owned land and surplus school properties for affordable housing projects; (3) codeveloper with local nonprofit and for-profit developers; (4) equity investor in nonprofit housing developments; and (5) supplier of technical assistance and seed money to cover early and soft costs of projects that will be built by other local nonprofit groups. BRIDGE has the strong backing of local businesses and has raised nearly $6 million from corporations and foundations for its revolving capital fund.

While extremely significant, the combined effort of these state and local, public and private efforts to provide low-cost housing "represents only a small fraction of the body of federal programs that this activity is trying to replace," Stegman and Holden warn. "The gap might narrow in the future, as more places mount local housing efforts. But without a substantial federal housing production presence, urgent needs will continue to outstrip available resources by a wide margin."

The Administration has pretty much taken a hands-off approach, suggesting that a response to the crisis should come at the local level and from the private as well as the public sector. This trend has been fueled by the severe federal budget deficit. On the federal level the Reagan Administration has lead Congess out of the housing business—HUD's budget dropped from $35.7 billion in fiscal year 1980 to $7 billion in fiscal year 1988. Also damaging, say critics, is the Reagan Administration's approach to housing—that of massive cuts and a move away from deep subsidies for housing and production of housing to vouchers. Critics argue that neither the public nor private sector will be able to assure a substantial amount of housing for the homeless or those with little means.

Concern about the homelessness crisis, however, has come from members of Congress. In December 1982, the House subcommittee on housing and community development held the first Congressional hearings on homelessness. In 1983 the Emergency Food and Shelter Program was created under the auspices of the Federal Emergency Management Agency and $100 million appropriated. Intended as only a one-year program, Congress has appropriated supplemental funding each year through fiscal year 1988. Nearly $500 million has been distributed to shelters and soup kitchens for food, supplies, equipment, rent and utility assistance, and minor rehabilitations. At the same time, local governments were encouraged to use Community Development Action Grant funds for shelter development, and through HUD's "Homes for the Homeless," foreclosed FHA properties are leased to nonprofit organizations for use as transitional housing.

The strongest acknowledgment of the homeless crisis by Congress to date is the passage of the Stewart B. McKinney Homeless Assistance Act in June 1987, and subsequently the appropriation of $442.7 million for fiscal years 1987 and $617 million for fiscal year 1988. A myriad of programs for social services, job training, food, and shelter comprise the act. Ones pertaining to housing are the Emergency Food and Shelter Program, the emergency Shelter Grant Program, Supportive Housing Demonstration Program, and Section 8 assistance for single-room-occupancy dwellings. These housing programs together receive approximately 50 percent of each years' appropriation. The McKinney Act also created an Inter-Agency Council on the Homeless and required that state and local governments submit a comprehensive homeless assistance plan prior to receiving any funding.

Meanwhile the role of state governments in providing assistance for homeless persons is increasing. In a survey of state activity Mary K. Nenno, of the National Association of Housing and Redevelopment Officials, found that 21 states have programs for the homeless that are not dependent on federal funding. Such programs include assistance with security deposits, rental assistance, support services, shelter operating assistance, rehabilitation of shelters, and new construction or substantial rehabilitation of buildings for transitional and permanent housing.

In *Assistance for Homeless Persons*, a NAHRO resource book, Nenno is both optimistic and pessimist toward these programs: "Many new states have initiated homeless assistance efforts over the past two years, and existing state programs are expanding," she writes. "To date, however, state homeless assistance, as is the case in federal or local homeless assistance, tends to be short-term and often lacks coordination. Only one state—Massachusetts—appears to be developing a coordinated homeless effort among the state departments and agencies that are concerned with homelessness."[11]

The Massachusetts program is conducted in several agenices, principally the executive office of communications and development and the departments of public welfare, social services, and mental health. Within the preview of these departments are the welfare program, rental subsidies to homeless persons, housing and residential services program for the mentally ill, a transitional housing program for pregnant and parenting teenagers, transitional housing for homeless families, a program to prevent homelessness, a housing innovations fund that provides loans and grants for development of "alternative housing," and a housing voucher program for homeless families.

Through her survey of local housing and community development agencies, Nenno found that "most of the documented efforts by the local agencies are single or one-time actions, usually of modest size. The number of housing units is fairly small, although in smaller communities, even a small number can represent a significant contribution." The reasons are two-fold, Nenno suggests: limited financial resources and lack of a federal program providing long-term aid for the homeless or for shelters for the homeless.

Examples of local programs for housing the homeless that Nenno found are:
• The Seattle Housing Authority (SHA) leases 45 public housing units for use as emergency housing. It runs a 230-bed emergency shelter and a 205-unit SRO in the same building downtown. SHA also purchased and renovated an existing building into a

17-unit emergency shelter and a 16-unit SRO.
• The Philadelphia Housing Development Corporation received a HUD grant for the rehabilitation of My Brother's House by the shelter's owner and operator. Ten percent of the $127,625 loan will be forgiven each year for ten years. The emergency shelter for homeless men is in downtown Philadelphia.
• The Cuyahoga Metropolitian Housing Authority's proposal to convert a 76-room motel in Cleveland into an emergency and transitional facility for battered and homeless women was approved by HUD and the Cuyahoga Metropolitan Housing Authority's Board of Commissioners only after a protracted battle with a prominent elected official who did not want the shelter built.
• In Iowa City, Iowa, the community development agency received federal Community Development Block Grant funds to acquire and rehabilitate an emergency shelter.
• The Memphis Housing Authority administers rental programs for low-income individuals who would not ordinarily qualify for housing assistance. It also provides transitional housing for women in 20 public housing units.

These and similar activities are taking place throughout the country in addition to the traditional aid for the homeless offered by churches, the Salvation Army, the Rescue Missions, to name a few. The mushrooming of new groups helping the homeless over the last half decade only reflects the magnitude of the homelessness crisis. Yet the need continues to far outstrip the remedies. The individuals that aid the homeless—and that see the human faces behind the homeless masks on a daily basis—wonder why this nation of such riches continues to overlook those among us who suffer the most.

Sometimes optimism in the future is maintained. Robert Hayes, of the National Coalition for the Homeless, said in 1986, "It seems that more and more people are recognizing homelessness as something that we the people through the government must deal with. . . . If there is any promise of a turn around in homelessness, which would necessitate a turn around in public resources going into housing the poor people, it will be because 51 percent of the American people have said, 'Enough.'" At other times the fight seems endless and small victories seem ephemeral.

The battle for decent housing for every American needs the support of people in all walks of life. Particularly welcomed is the involvement of professionals whose skills and talents can have direct bearing on easing the crisis.

Photographs by Ray Mortenson

# THE SEARCH FOR SHELTER

Particularly sensitive to the expanding housing crisis are professionals whose work had some relationship to the problem—architects, developers, lawyers, urban planners, social workers, psychiatrists, doctors, and others. In larger and larger numbers these professionals have begun to acknowledge their own contributions to the crisis and offer solutions to alleviate the suffering. This awakening of social consciousness continues today.

An early leader of this movement was the American Psychiatric Association (APA). In 1984 the APA task force on the homeless mentally ill pointed to well-intended decisions made by the psychiatric community that contributed significantly to the homeless crisis in America. Central to the controversy was the deinstitutionalization of the chronically mentally ill, which began in the early 1950s. By 1985 there were 150,000 patients in state mental institutions, compared with 500,000 in 1950.

"The concept of deinstitutionalization per se was not bad," the APA task force reported. "The idea that many, if not most, of the severely and chronically mentally ill suffering from serious illnesses such as schizophrenia and manic-depression could be cared for in community programs rather than in institutions was clinically sound and economically feasible. The way deinstitutionalization was originally carried out, however, through the poorly planned discharge of thousands of mentally ill residents of state hospitals into inadequately prepared or programmatically deficient communities, was another thing altogether." By 1980 the goal of establishing 2,000 community mental-health centers nationwide was 1,300 short.

What was, and still is, needed are "an adequate number and range of community residential settings, with varying degrees of supervision and structure; a system of follow-up, monitoring, and responsibility for ensuring that services are provided to those unable to obtain them; and easy access to short-term and long-term inpatient care when indicated. The consequences of these gaps in essential resources have been disastrous," the APA task force stated. Many

of those chronically mentally ill eventually ended up on the streets.

For the architectural profession, the awakening process began when the number of homeless people on the streets of cities throughout the country was increasing dramatically. Architects began to acknowledge that they had been "part of a process of reasoned solutions for community revitalization that has been a contributing factor to the increase in homelessness," reflects Blake Chambliss, FAIA, of Anderson Mason and Dale in Denver. Perhaps most visible was the elimination of more than one million units of low-cost housing—old hotels, boarding homes, and inner-city apartments—through urban renewal, abandonment, arson, and gentrification. Few, if any, of these low-cost units were replaced.

As Conrad Levenson, whose New York City architectural firm specializes in low-cost housing, said in 1985, "In city after city, the homeless are gathered in the streets, bused to gymnasiums, armories, and church basements for a night's sleep in spaces jammed with cots. In the morning they return to the streets again to wander in search of warmth, food, or a public bathroom until evening comes. It is now clear that the homeless population is rapidly growing and that long-term housing solutions will not come next winter or the winters that will soon follow. Quality shelter must be provided. And who more than architects should be concerned and involved in the creation of shelter?"

To examine more closely these issues and others, the AIA housing committee held two symposia in 1985—one in Portland, Ore., a city that was actively searching for solutions, and the other in Washington, D.C., where lawmakers were beginning to address the homelessness crisis. Invited to these meetings were local, state, and federal government officials, housing experts, advocates for the homeless, and even the homeless themselves. At the AIA annual convention later that year, delegates supported the development of a resource guide on housing the homeless, ultimately published under the title *The Search for Shelter* (the companion publication of this book).

113

# THE SEARCH FOR SHELTER

In a somewhat different way that awakening continues today. "Recently I fretted over a condominium project we were working on in New Jersey," says Herbert Oppenheimer, FAIA, of the New York City architecture firm Oppenheimer & Vogelstein. "Were the dimensions of the swimming pool correct? How about the health club and other luxury items? Where they adequate? Shortly thereafter I was asked by a citizen's committee to review plans for a homeless shelter that had already been approved by the city and state. In that shelter 30 people—men, women, and children—would be sleeping in one room. The plans called for no operable, full-size windows, only a few clerestories.... When comparing the two projects, it become quite evident to me that the split between architecture for the rich and architecture for the poor is more pronounced than ever."

As Oppenheimer discovered, the most destitute in this country exist in an environment that is devoid of almost all the qualities associated with decent, humane living conditions: There is little privacy, little sense of belonging, and inadequate ventilation, bathroom facilities, and natural lighting. Rather than a domestic ambience, the overall character is institutional, and it is institutional at its worst—the warehousing of human beings.

Two examples: A city-run emergency shelter for men and women in Seattle is entered through a door off the back alley, an attempt to keep the street people separated from the well-heeled professionals working in that part of town. The shelter has two large, open rooms for male "guests" and one for the females. When full the shelter accommodates some 230 people sleeping on mats just inches apart. This sleeping arrangement might be considered adequate as a short-term refuge after some natural disaster; it is inconceivable that some have resided there for months. Multiply this scene five times and place it in an armory gymnasium, and you have the Fort Washington Shelter in New York City. That shelter for 1,000 men is frightening in its disregard for human dignity; and our society is monstrously negligent for allowing such an atrocity to exist.

As architects began to see this nightmare played out in cities across the country, it became obvious that their expertise was needed not only in providing decent, humane environments but also in vehemently protesting the inhumane conditions that exist for the homeless. Architecture critic Paul Goldberger wrote in the March 27, 1988, *New York Times*: "It has not been particularly fashionable for architects to care about social problems lately; for most of the last generation, this has given way to more esthetic preoccupations. Now there are clear signs that architects are willing, even eager, to turn their talents toward social concerns."

All the while it was becoming more and more apparent that the tragedy of homelessness was only the tip of a much broader low-cost housing crisis. That architects could aid in the delivery of housing for the homeless—whether emergency, transitional, or permanent housing—was already acknowledged. "Architects by training and instinct have a natural interest in this problem. Our training shows us how to provide shelter. Our instinct fosters that creative urge to leave this world a better place than we found it," says former AIA president Donald Hackl, FAIA. And there was evidence that providers of housing and services for the homeless needed design professionals to supervise the planning, design, renovation, and construction of shelters, particularly if those shelters hoped to receive city, state, and/or federal funding. Architects could indeed become leaders in the fight against homelessness.

Just how architects could get involved was not clear, however. So the Search for Shelter program was established to provide a process for architects to join with others in addressing a particular housing problem in their community. Sponsored by the American Institute of Architects (AIA), the American Institute of Architecture Students (AIAS), and the Neighborhood Reinvestment Corporation, this program calls for architects, architecture students and educators, housing providers and advocates, government officials, builders, financiers, community activists, church and civic leaders, and others

in a community to join forces to undertake projects like the following:
• design shelters and low-cost housing for the homeless and others with little means;
• study the effects of codes and standards on housing costs and quality;
• find ways to use zoning ordinances to bring low-cost housing to a neighborhood rather than exclude it and work to gain community support for such an initiative;
• participate in the drafting of new local, state, and federal housing legislation;
• organize a city-wide symposium to address the local housing problems.

The Search for Shelter's overall goals are broader than designing new shelters; expanding the dialogue on what is appropriate long-term housing for people with little means is also of great importance.

The triad forged between the sponsors represents a tremendous wealth of knowledge, skills, and resources that could potentially be brought to bear upon the housing crisis. As a professional association, AIA has over 50,000 members nationwide, members that represent architect-practitioners, but also architect-developers, architect-legislators, and architect-educators. Founded it 1867, AIA's purpose is "to promote the esthetic, scientific, and practical efficiency of the architectural profession; to advance the science and art of planning and buildings; to coordinate the building industry and the profession to improve the environment; and to make the profession of ever-increasing service to society." Besides the national headquarters, there are nearly 300 local, state, and regional chapters.

The AIAS brings its network of students and college and university chapters—an approximate 35,000 architecture students in over 135 schools. In addition, the AIAS groups maintain a strong connection with architectural educators. The AIAS goal is to "prepare architecture students to enter the profession of architecture, to promote excellence in design, academic enrichment, and student-practitioner interaction, as well as to foster an

appreciation of architecture and related disciplines among all persons." To the triad, the students bring a refreshing enthusiasm to succeed and the energy needed to accomplish hard tasks. Their quest for deeper knowledge and new solutions can be infectious.

Neighborhood Reinvestment was chartered by the U.S. Congress in 1978 to maintain and expand a successful system for neighborhood revitalization in this country. Its goal is neighborhood revitalization through housing development and rehabilitation, commercial revitalization and economic development, stablized real estate markets, and renewed neighborhood pride. Its network includes nonprofit community development organizations in some 130 cities. These community organizations, generally referred to as Neighborhood Housing Services, bring to the Search for Shelter triad an intimate understanding of a particular city's or community's housing ills, what opportunities or barriers may be encountered when introducing new housing for the homeless or those with little means, and how to engage a public commitment for a project.

Combined, representatives of these three groups comprise a powerful coalition for better low-cost housing. And in itself the interchange between the players is gratifying: the Neighborhood Reinvestment groups may gain a better understanding of the benefits of good design and also have some valuable suggestions for the designers; architects can assume a leadership role in addressing a community's problems but also increase their own understanding of the users' needs; and in their interaction with the architect-practitioners, the community development organizations, and the potential housing tenants, the students can gain invaluable insights on this "real-world" experience.

From its inception, then, the Search for Shelter showed promise of being an excellent "approach or process through which we can form partnerships on a local and national level and move ahead," as Donald Hackl, FAIA, the president of AIA for

115

# THE SEARCH FOR SHELTER

1987, suggested. In each community the program sponsors would work to gain support from other professionals.

Because of this community orientation, the results of the first 29 workshops are as diverse as the cities—and the communities—in which they were held. For instance the two projects in New York City, a city that for years has been vigorously combating homelessness, differ greatly from those in smaller towns, such as Shreveport, La., where the public is just becoming aware of its homelessness problems. (A closer examination of the Search for Shelter results begins on page 12.)

A main premise of the Search for Shelter is that no specialized group can solve the nation's housing ills but that coalitions must be formed in the community to develop solutions to particular local housing problems. In the Dec. 26, 1987, *Washington Post* architecture critic Benjamin Forgey described the Search for Shelter as "at once a modest and farsighted attempt to bring together the energies and talents of architectural students, working professionals, and a host of agencies and individuals grappling with the problem of the homeless. With an idealism chastened by the failure of so much large-scale public housing in the postwar period (and also by the obvious lack of money for housing in the Reagan era), the AIA program consciously abjured the big, predetermined solution, choosing instead to respond 'to people rather than abstract ideas,' in the words of former AIA president Donald Hackl, FAIA."

The first step of the Search for Shelter process, therefore, is the formation of a steering committee consisting of members of that broad coalition of community players—anyone who has a potential role in the planning, construction, and maintenence of shelters or long-term, low-cost housing. Hand in hand with the formation of this new coalition is the assessment of the community's existing services and housing opportunities—for both the homeless and the near homeless. Then the initial questions can begin.

Have the community's needs and resources been surveyed? If not, what organizations can aid in the research? What population is most in need of housing—single women with children, the chronically mentally ill, single men? Should the Search for Shelter coalition direct its activities to a specific building project, or is increasing the community's awareness of the need for more permanent, low-cost housing a more urgent need? Do local building codes and standards and zoning respond to the housing crisis by, for instance, classifying SROs? Are neighborhoods using zoning laws to keep out shelters or low-cost housing? Is new legislation at the city or state level needed to direct more dollars to the development of low-cost housing? Are any SROs in need of a new management plan? How closely are the community's social services tied to the shelters for the homeless and low-cost housing? Is day care provided?

The majority of the first Search for Shelter workshops (most were held during October 1987) concentrated on shelter design. The leaders were mainly architects who have spent much of their careers in housing or community development. Other leaders surfaced, however—a developer in Shreveport, La.; a housing expert in Phoenix; a Neighborhood Housing Services director in Ithaca, N.Y.; and an architecture educator in New Orleans.

The process of choosing the projects varied. In Pittsburgh, for example, rather than identifying a particular building that could be renovated into a shelter, the task force worked with existing shelter providers, developing feasible options for renovation or expansion of existing facilities. In all, five shelter groups participated in the Pittsburgh workshop; the projects range from an emergency shelter for homeless men to a transitional shelter for battered women and their children.

Elsewhere:

• In Shreveport, La., a developer wanted to save an old hotel located at the edge of a historic district and opposite a depressed business corridor. The

hotel was to be renovated for low-income housing, most likely as an SRO facility. This developer learned of the Search for Shelter program and saw it as a way to get the community—and the city as a whole—behind the project. Events there led to the mayor making his first public acknowledgment of the homeless problem in Shreveport. The newly renovated McAdoo Hotel opened its doors to single men and women on Aug. 28, 1988.
• The Baltimore Search for Shelter team identified specific homeless populations in need of shelter, as well as buildings that could be renovated for specific shelter groups. Among the five projects are the transformation of a block of abandoned row houses into affordable housing and the renovation of an elementary school into a shelter for families.
• In Syracuse the gentrification of an older neighborhood was encroaching on a dilapidated residential hotel. If the building was to be renovated into more up-scale condominiums, the 150 residents would have to leave. The Syracuse Search for Shelter team took as its goal the renovation of the hotel into an SRO.
• In Brooklyn deliberately mixing populations—the elderly with teenage mothers and their children—is meant to encourage interaction, with the hope that "foster" parent and grandparent relationships will grow.
    Some groups, however, took different approaches:
• The Boulder, Colo., team studied the housing currently available to the chronically mentally ill in the city. The intent was twofold: to determine what type of housing was offered—group homes, SROs, apartments, or more institutional settings—and then eventually to design new shelters or make recommendations to others providing new shelters.
• One group from the Denver Search for Shelter task force traveled north to the town of Brighton to study whether a housing organization should enlarge its current shelter (a schoolhouse), relocate to a large warehouse, or build a new facility. Sixteen criteria were devised for the evaluation.
• The Lexington, Ky., Search for Shelter team

studied low-cost housing in rural Appalachia.
• In Los Angeles a competition called for the design of a new village of transitional housing for 64 persons on a 30,000-square-foot lot.
• In New Orleans the result was more theoretical: a network of mobile units that by day would reach out into the community and by night would return to an empty warehouse and become sleeping quarters; a three-dimensional billboard meant to provoke a public response to the crisis; and city sleepers (individual, portable sleeping capsules).
    Regardless of the topic of study, each Search for Shelter group was encouraged to hold a forum and invite the general public. Design workshops lasted from one day to a week in duration. Specifics of the workshops varied significantly.
    Raising public awareness of the plight of the homeless and the unsuitable housing conditions in which those with little means survive is similar to tossing a stone into the water and waiting. Sometimes the ripples broaden quickly, sometimes not. In some cities the Search for Shelter workshop caused the first waves; in others it merely kept in motion ripples already made.
    A good perpetuator of ripples is the local news media. The largest waves were perhaps made in Shreveport, La. There, the workshop was held July 22-25, 1987, and since it was the first Search for Shelter effort it became the pilot project. As indicated in the following chronology, the local media became both a means to publicize the Shreveport workshop but also to broaden the debate over whether the poor are being adequately housed in that city.
• May 7, 1987: *The Shreveport Journal* announces the Search for Shelter project that will develop renovation plans for the McAdoo Hotel and also "draw attention to the homeless and to housing needs in Shreveport."
• May 7, 1987: A *Journal* editorial observes: "People seen sleeping under bridges and in abandoned buildings locally are signs that Shreveport has not escaped the national scourge of homelessness. For-

tunately, the city now has the opportunity to open its first homeless shelter if a proposed renovation project goes as planned. . . . Although 42 rooms will only begin to address the needs of the homeless in Shreveport, this form of public/private initiative will lay the groundwork for further homeless projects both locally and nationwide. Shreveport should rally behind the McAdoo renovation; it's the type of project the city needs more of in hard economic times."

• July 10, 1987: Both the *Journal* and the *Shreveport Times* announce the workshop schedule.

• July 19, 1987: The *Times* publishes an article analyzing substandard housing, the first of a series of articles on the city's housing situation. "Living in a house with faulty wiring and no bathroom is a nightmare. A nightmare that Henrietta Thomas and her three sons lived for about three and one-half years before waking up and moving out. 'It was terrible living there. The electricity was all messed up. But it was only $50-a-month rent, and that's all I could afford,' Ms. Thomas said. A welfare recipient, she said her meager income kept her 'trapped in a nightmare' in the substandard Shreveport housing."

• July 19, 1987: The *Times* gives more details of the Search for Shelter workshop.

• July 20, 1987: The second article of a *Times* series examines "Housing Projects: A World of Contrast."

• July 21, 1987: A *Journal* article announces the arrival of architecture students from Louisiana Tech University, who will participate in the Search for Shelter. They will "be housed at the Creswell Hotel [an existing SRO] here, will eat a meal at the Hospitality House [a soup kitchen], and will take a walking tour of the neighborhood near the old McAdoo Hotel."

• July 23, 1987: The *Times* reports on the Shreveport Search for Shelter public forum: "The homeless problem is close to home. That realization comes quickly when listening to the directors of local refuge homes complain of having to turn battered women away. Or when listening to a mother cry because her mentally ill son cannot support himself and cannot find a place able to keep him. Mayor John Hussey said he was unaware of a homeless problem in Shreveport until he became involved in a design workshop for housing the homeless. . . . Shreveport's many social programs have 285 beds available while more than 1,600 people have been turned away, he said."

• July 23, 1987: "At Least 1,000 People Homeless in Shreveport," a *Journal* headline reads.

• July 25, 1987: The *Times* reports, "The historic McAdoo Hotel will get an estimated $600,000 facelift, and Shreveport's homeless will get a first-rate facility that will cater to their needs, said Mary Nesbitt of Nesbitt Management. . . . 'I couldn't have said that before this project started,' said Nesbitt, whose company has an option to buy the McAdoo."

• July 26, 1987: The third article of the *Times* series states, "It is one of those perennial problems that are difficult enough to fully grasp and harder still to solve. Substandard housing has long been one of the major challenges for Shreveport. Thousands of Shreveport residents live in dilapidated houses, sometimes with no running water, no ceiling over their heads or with no peace from rats and vermin."

• July 26, 1987: A *Times* columnist ponders the problem in an article entitled "Housing and the Homeless, Right Here at Home."

• July 27, 1987: A *Journal* article under the headline "Workshop on Homeless Here Praised as Awakening to Problem" states: "Shreveport had a crash course on its homeless problem this past week."

Obviously, such enthusiasm is not a likely response in cities that are already addressing the homeless crisis; yet, important progress can be made there also. Take Chicago, for example: The Search for Shelter forum discussions among an alderman, representatives of the city's housing and planning departments, a resident of a local mission, a woman who started her own shelter, and prominent architects, among others, led to a citywide re-examination of the Chicago building codes that work against the development of affordable housing, particularly SROs. "The Search for Shelter certainly opened up a lot of eyes in the Chicago architectural community and the local government. It was very unique in that respect," says John Tomassi, AIA, the organizer of the city's Search for Shelter efforts and director of the Chicago Architectural Assistance Center.

In Pontiac, Mich., the Search for Shelter task force received a mayoral acknowledgment: Mayor Walter Moore resolved that the formation of the task force produced a "strong sense of achievement" and that the city supported "this collaborative effort of providing secure, welcoming housing to help restore the pride and dignity of homeless people and assist them in their return to independent living."

At the Washington, D.C., forum Mayor Marion Barry stated emphatically, "We're going to lose the war on homelessness unless everybody gets involved in the war. We can make a difference with this program." In the nation's capital the Search for Shelter team will transform a boarded up, dilapidated row house into a warm, inviting home for women.

Search for Shelter activities also acted as a catalyst in other ways. Fred Karnas, director of the Community Housing Partnership, Inc., in Phoenix and leader of the city's Search for Shelter effort, wrote: "On Jan. 4 [1988] the Community Housing Partnership (CHP) will close on the purchase of the vacant nursing home, one of the facilities studied during the Search for Shelter workshop. CHP received word in early December that it would receive over $1 million in HUD funding during a 10-year period to rehabilitate the property and provide Section 8 certificates for the 31 SRO tenants who will be living there. . . . I believe the Search for Shelter workshop played a key role in the success of the CHP and City of Phoenix Neighborhood Improvement and Housing Department proposal to HUD."

As of early October 1988, nineteen Search for Shelter projects have or will be built, many funded partially with money generated by the federal Stewart McKinney Act. Other projects will likely be funded and built in the future.

For others, the Search for Shelter project had more personal meaning. In the Nov. 7, 1987, *Washington Post* architect Roger K. Lewis, FAIA, wrote of the Baltimore workshop: "In many ways, the most fascinating aspect of the workshop experience was entering temporarily the invisible, easily ignored world of the homeless. . . . Our week-long 'search for shelter' revealed what statistics and headlines don't show. We learned that no matter how diverse their individual circumstances, what the homeless have in common is the street and the status of becoming the nation's 'untouchables.'"

For students who participated, the Search for Shelter was an eye-opening experience. "While a sense of architectural vision was established, perhaps the exercise was most important in that many young designers were sensitized to a world that none of them had come from and none of them live in yet exists all about them in a city such as Baltimore," suggests a Neighborhood Design Center spokesperson. (NDC was a partner in the Baltimore Search for Shelter.)

A social conscience is re-awakening. "Throughout the week, I experienced a kind of deja vu about this project," Roger Lewis continues. "It recalled the socially conscious agenda that preoccupied so many architects, and much of the public, during the 1960s, an agenda that was largely abandoned in the 1970s and 1980s when designers tended to pursue architecture more as a visual art than a social art. Yet the shelter problem continues and may be worse than ever before."

Despite this growing response by those in the building and design community, difficulties remain. In planning many of the Search for Shelter workshops, the recruitment of professionals to participate was the most bothersome task. This difficulty could have been caused by logistical and organizational problems, but it also raises some serious questions. Are architects and other professionals so burdened by keeping their practices alive that spare time is a precious commodity? Are they reluctant to get involved in any project as volunteers rather than a paid workers? Would they be willing to participate in such projects on an at-cost basis? How about as a volunteer on a one-project basis? Do serious liability problems arise, particularly if the Search for Shelter project leads to working drawings and then construction? Do architects and other professionals lack compassion?

One force that has persisted through the ebb and flow of the nation's social conscience is the network of community design centers (CDCs) scattered across the country. Now 35 strong, CDCs are nonprofit groups consisting of design, development, management, and advocacy professionals (and are not to be confused with community development corporations). One of the first CDCs was founded in 1964 by a group of architects in New York City, the Architects Renewal Committee, formed to aid Harlem residents in combating construction of a proposed freeway and other unwanted "improvements" in their community. The underlying theme has been that communities should—and do—have a right to participate in planning their own environments.

During the 1980s many CDCs have turned their attention to the affordable housing crisis. And during those first Search for Shelter workshops six CDCs played pivotal roles: the Chicago Architectural Assistance Center; Pratt Architectural Collaborative in Brooklyn, N.Y.; Baltimore's Neighborhood Design Assistance Center; the Design Planning Assistance Center in Albuquerque, N.M.; the Columbus (Ohio) Neighborhood Design Assistance Center; and the East Tennessee Community Design Center in Knoxville. Forming coalitions to design and build housing, as well as other community projects, is part of the CDC goal and is seen by some as a strong point of the Search for Shelter program. "That program has been successful because it has focused on the fact that it is not architects alone but rather a collaborative effort that puts a facility together—the architects, users, service providers, community, financial packagers, government representatives, and developers," says Pratt's Cindy Harden, leader of the Brooklyn workshop.

These CDCs will continue their community work after the Search for Shelter projects are completed. It appears likely that several other Search for Shelter groups will remain together after their initial projects: The purpose may be simply to follow through or they may expand their efforts. Some could join an existing community design center, create new ones, or set up a clearinghouse for professionals wishing to contribute to such projects in the future—whether pro bono, at cost, or for a more typical fee.

Such services undoubtedly are needed, but, again, there is concern that not enough professionals support these "socially conscious" endeavors. Kathleen Dorgan, director of the Capitol Hill Improvement Albany Center Corporation in Albany, N.Y., has witnessed the closing of four of the seven CDCs in that state. "I'm saddened that a lot of the community design centers have closed over the last several years," she says, "particularly since we are beginning to rethink how to design and deliver low-income housing and how that housing fits into the community. If, as a profession, we architects let people decide that low-income housing is done better without us, it is very hard for us to make the argument that other kinds of community projects will benefit from our services."

Yet, the overall momentum is toward more positive participation in formal or informal searches for shelter. In Seattle, for example, a city-sponsored competition in early 1988 calling for creative ways to build affordable housing downtown brought entries from more than 400 architects, developers, and other housing specialists. On weekends in Atlanta, architects, industrial designers, bank employees, and other professionals turn into the Mad Housers, erecting huts around town for the homeless. Their ultimate goal is twofold: to embarrass the city government into taking action regarding the city's homeless and, until the city does, to provide a place for some of these homeless to live.

Other design professionals are dealing with the housing crisis in less boisterous ways. In November 1986 architect Leonard J. Currie, FAIA, of Blacksburg, Va., opened a free architecture clinic to be held each Saturday morning. Currie's goal is to "provide limited architectural services to local urban or rural property owners of limited means who cannot afford professional advice in planning improvements or enhancements of their homes." Of the housing shortage in Appalachia, Currie says, "The federal government, with the burgeoning deficit as an excuse, has cut back so severely that a federal program ceases to exist. More is left to the private sector."

Still others are searching for answers to the housing crisis in ways similar to the Search for Shelter. Take the New York Chapter of Architects, Designers, and Planners for Social Responsibility: In 1987 more than 250 students and 14 faculty from colleges around New York City spent a weekend to a semester planning and designing housing for the homeless.

Peter Marcuse, a professor of urban planning at Columbia University's Graduate School of Architecture, Planning, and Preservation, says through this process "we can enlighten others and ourselves about the homeless as we try to detail housing for them. We can show that their needs are essentially all of ours—they want a community, social support, public services, security, friendship, space, and privacy. Our buildings can show that the homeless need not be isolated, but can be integrated into our society. . . .

"We can design housing that is flexible, where people can feel like individuals, instead of an undifferentiated mass. Even if we find it necessary to design what are called 'emergency shelters,' we can acknowledge that the homeless will return there many times, and provide as much of a 'home' as we can—at least a place to leave belongings during the day, and provide a setting for socializing at night. . . .

"The buildings we propose for the homeless should sustain the criteria expected in all our work. If we deliberately lower our standards for the homeless and develop housing types suitable only for them, we will only intensify the stigma they bear, he adds."[1]

Marcuse suggests, and the Search for Shelter results indicate, that further investigation must be made into precisely what is decent housing for the homeless and those with little means. Are standards changing? For better or worse? Can new technologies provide housing of similar quality but at much less cost? Is it no longer acceptable to ostracize the poorest in this country in isolated ghettos or massive subsidized housing complexes? Should mixed neighborhoods, where the poor live alongside the rich, be encouraged? Answers to these and other questions are yet to come.

# LOW-COST HOUSING REDEFINED

The housing crisis has caused and will continue to cause misery for hundreds of thousands of Americans, if not more. Yet, out of this crisis has come an energetic examination of housing policy and development practices in this country. The outcome promises to be an approach to low-cost housing that is radically different—in both design and delivery—from earlier times.

But first, semantics: Homelessness is easily described—it simply means being without a home. It refers not only to those living on the streets but also to the hidden homeless—"guests" of shelters for the homeless or people doubling up with friends or relatives. Describing housing as low-cost, low-income, or affordable can cause confusion. Generally such housing is occupied by persons of low or no income who more often than not receive a public subsidy to help cover housing costs. But the meaning of the term *affordable housing* is deceptive because in a wealthy community such housing is usually beyond the means of the poorer population. The general rule of thumb is that a household should not spend more than 30 percent of gross household income for all shelter costs. Shelter can describe housing for the homeless, but it also can be synonymous with the generic definition of housing.

Regardless of income, a common thread binds all home owners and renters and even the homeless themselves—the desire for a decent home in a decent community. "We can enlighten ourselves and others about the homeless as we try to detail housing for them. We can show that their needs are essentially all of ours—they want a community, social support, public services, security, friendship, space, privacy. The homeless need not be isolated, but can be integrated into our society. We can design housing that is flexible, where people can feel like individuals, instead of an undifferentiated mass," says Peter Marcuse, professor of urban planning at Columbia University's graduate school of architecture, planning, and preservation. "The homeless should be involved in their design and consulted about their needs, as should any other client.

The buildings we propose for them should sustain the criteria expected in all our work. If we deliberately lower our standards for the homeless and develop housing types suitable just for them, we will only intensify the stigma they bear."[1]

Over the years low-cost housing has failed to satisfy the expectations set forth by Marcuse. While recognized as well-intended efforts to eliminate substandard housing, the urban renewal practices of the 1950s and 1960s are now credited with creating a new type of ghetto, one of much greater magnitude. Entire inner-city slum neighborhoods were bulldozed and replaced by huge, subsidized housing developments. Cut off from the surrounding neighborhoods, these new superghettoes became bastions of poverty, crime, and squalor; the worst of these superghettoes was Pruitt-Igoe, built close to downtown St. Louis in the late 1950s. Pruitt-Igoe with its 12,000 tenants in a cluster of high-rise buildings soon became the symbol of a misguided social housing policy. The complex was eventually blown to bits. By the 1970s the superblock concept gave way to the idea of smaller subsidized housing developments—duplexes and garden apartments.

But other problems persisted. Established in the 1960s the federal government's Section 236 program offered developers one percent mortgage loans, lucrative tax breaks and, in some cases, rent subsidies to build and manage low-income housing. But developers were not encouraged to adequately manage and maintain the units. By the 1970s corruption and default were rampant. In 1973 President Nixon froze all Section 236 housing starts and in 1974 created the Section 8 program.

The Section 8 program was built on the Section 236 premise of a public-private partnership, but under Section 8 tenants, rather than owners of housing, would receive vouchers to supplement the amount of rent they could afford and the market rent. Incentives were also given to developers of housing, although the volume dropped tremendously. According to economic writer Robert Kuttner in the April 25, 1988, edition of *The New Republic*, there are two major flaws of the Section 8 program: "First, it didn't build enough new housing. By giving poor people more purchasing power it only bid up rent levels. Second, it was a one-way deal. A landlord could accept Section 8 tenants as long as his neighborhood was depressed, but as soon as the neighborhood became a candidate for gentrification, the landlord could quit the subsidized market for the free market." Today under Section 236 and Section 8 there are nearly three million housing units. But, as explained in Chapter One, a significant number of those units may be lost in the near future as contracts with the federal government expire.

A fairly consistent source of housing since the New Deal era is public housing built and owned by the federal government. Currently there are approximately 1.4 million public housing units operated by local public housing authorities, with the operating subsidies supplied by the federal government. While some are of the same vintage as Pruitt-Igoe, most are smaller-scale garden apartments. Isolation remains a problem. "Public housing once served the working poor; but since the 1960s it has become home to the hardest core of the poor," writes Kuttner. In the 1980s Congress and the Reagan Administration have halted construction of any new public housing. More damaging, perhaps, is the lack of funding for badly needed renovations—as much as $25 billion, a HUD-commissioned study found.

In reaction against the megaslums of the 1950s and 1960s, architects and others in the development community began to "discuss urban planning and urban design as well as good design. When we talked about 'social housing,' we were concerned not only with finding a means to provide affordable housing, but also with the need to connect this housing with the design of the rest of the city to create new, or to reinforce existing, neighborhoods, not disrupt and destroy them," says Lewis Davis, a partner of the New York City architecture firm Davis Brody.[2]

Yet, knitting such projects into a neighborhood was—and is—no easy task. Integrating housing for the homeless and low-income housing can seem nearly impossible. Such housing has traditionally been located in undesirable locations isolated from the rest of the community. "The difficulty of obtaining public acceptance of homeless housing in neighborhoods has led the city [and likewise county, state, and private organizations] to select less desirable sites in remote locations," suggests Conrad Levenson, whose New York City-based architecture firm concentrates on designing and developing low- and very low-income housing. "Homelessness creates a desperate sense of loss and isolation. Individuals and families in need of support should not be further isolated, by design, in antiseptic compounds remote from access to transportation, schools, shopping, recreation, and other positive features of community life," Levenson continues.

The housing crisis of the 1980s, however, is forcing the integration of low-cost housing into neighborhoods consisting mainly of middle- and upper-income neighborhoods, creating more socioeconomically diverse communities. This trend is fueled by economics: Renovating what is already built can prove substantially less costly—up to one-third less—than building anew. Given the magnitude of the housing crisis, every possible resource in cities and in the countryside needs to be tapped—buildings and vacant lots owned by a city through default, vacant lots owned by private developers who are willing to part with them at a low price in return for tax benefits or special development rights, or buildings that no longer serve their original functions and are vacant. Strong community resistance (known as NIMBY, for "not in my back yard") can magnify the need to weave the new low-cost housing into an existing neighborhood fabric.

An important source for increasing the housing supply has been identified—the "shadow market," a term coined by William C. Baer, an urban and regional planning professor at the University of

Southern California. Baer's premise is that a community's housing supply can expand significantly by renovation into residential units of buildings formerly used for nonresidential purposes (industrial lofts, schools, churches), former group quarters (sorority houses, convents), and units created by subdividing or adding to existing dwellings. This market accounted for one-third of the low-cost units occupied by owners and one-half of the units occupied by renters from 1973 to 1980, Baer maintains.

"To bring this 'shadow market' alive, local governments need only to make modest changes to building codes and zoning regulations," Baer suggests. "Housing policies of all kinds take physical form only after they have been processed through local building codes, zoning ordinances, and other regulations. Such regulations are often viewed less as housing policies than as land-use policies or as rules protecting the public's health, safety and welfare."

Shadow market properties under examination by the Search for Shelter teams included a warehouse, a vacant nursing home, a motel, a former group home for college students, a Moose lodge, a doctor's office and residence, and a hospital.

Developing shelters for the homeless and low-cost housing on a small scale at various locations in a community or city is considered scattered-site development. The Boston Housing Partnership, a nonprofit organization supported by the public and private sector, undertook one of the first large scattered-site development plans in 1983 by rehabilitating 700 housing units in 69 scattered-site apartment buildings. In Memphis, the Metropolitan Inter-Faith Association has renovated 10 HUD-owned properties on scattered sites for 60-day transitional shelter for homeless families.

In Phoenix the Search for Shelter team joined the city in examining whether scattered-site development for the homeless could be successful there. "As a total community, Phoenix is grappling with the concept of dispersed shelters for the homeless

population, the idea being that smaller facilities focused on the needs of sub-populations of the homeless would be more humane for the shelter guests and more palatable to the neighborhoods impacted by them," explains Fred Karnas, executive director of the Community Housing Partnership and leader of the Phoenix Search for Shelter project. "In addition, such a plan would equalize the impact of shelters throughout the community, reducing the argument that shelters, halfway houses, etc., are always located in certain vulnerable neighborhoods."

Another approach is to mix people of different income levels in the same housing development; thus, the monthly revenue generated by the market-rate units would help subsidize the low-cost ones. This strategy is more controversial than scattered-site development and is intrinsically tied to inclusionary zoning policies, zoning that through incentives encourages developers to include low- and moderate-income units in more traditionally "closed" housing developments (see chapter 2 for a more in-depth discussion of inclusionary zoning). Enacted in 1983, the Massachusetts State Housing Assistance Program for Rental Production (SHARP), for example, provides loans to local governments, housing authorities, and nonprofit organizations to develop rental housing projects with a minimum of 25 percent of the units reserved for low- and moderate-income tenants.

Massachusetts's SHARP housing has quite successfully mixed populations. In the SHARP apartment buildings "nobody knows who's what income, because all of the apartments are identical and tenants are distributed in a totally random pattern with no relationship to income or race," says Joan Goody, of the Boston architectural firm Goody, Clancy & Associates. "In the large mixed-income projects, the developers often have established counseling services to help families that have lived only in 'projects' to adjust to the new environment."

Overall, integrated projects and neighborhoods 125

can significantly benefit a community in physical form and human relations. "Individual dwellings must have some evident relation to a larger community," wrote Donlyn Lyndon, a professor of architecture at University of California at Berkeley and a partner of the architecture firm Lyndon/Buchanan in Berkeley. "To be prudent it makes more sense to fit new housing in among an existing community and weave a common place than to isolate and segregate new construction from old, subsidized or not. The contraints of a specific site become assets in the creation of identity," Lyndon adds.[3] Of the human aspect, Blake Chambliss, FAIA, of Anderson, Mason and Dale in Denver, believes that "the results of Neighborhood Reinvestment and Neighborhood Housing Services throughout the country have shown that when a community and a neighborhood work together in some sort of organized way, they can do a tremendous number of things that are not just housing."

When a community and neighborhood work together, the focus is transformed from a single project design into community design. "The first principle of community design is to recognize the rights of all citizens to have a voice in decisions that affect the places they inhabit, work, and linger in. Whatever the method, the goal has been to enable people to participate in their environment," says Mary Comerio, founder of the Community Design Center and Center for Environmental Change in Berkeley, Calif.

Crucial to the successful melding of new housing into an established neighborhood are the following design considerations:
• Scale. "This is where perhaps the modern movement really lost its way concerning social housing. Its adherents believed an enormous, heroic scale, like Pruitt-Igoe, was appropriate for low-income families. Now, we are working on a much smaller scale," says Herbert Oppenheimer, FAIA, of the New York City architecture firm Oppenheimer & Vogelstein.
• Physical relationships. The aim is to "connect

back to the neighborhood concerning the street system, the appearance of the building, the way people are organized within the building. For example, if the project is in a neighborhood that has a lot of townhouses, then in its renovation we try to create that townhouse feeling," Goody says. Comerio adds, "The design of housing and public places should involve the rational and poetic understanding of what makes a place work and what makes it special and significant."
• Materials. Brick public housing built in predominantly clapboard neighborhoods in Massachusetts, for example, sticks out like a sore thumb. "Thirty years ago in those neighborhoods the slums were torn down and replaced with red brick buildings. Every building was identical, so the red brick became associated with public housing projects. Now when we are renovating these buildings," Goody says, "we try to use more vernacular siding. We cover the brick with stucco or paint."

Regardless of what type of shelter is to be created—low-cost housing or emergency or transitional shelter for the homeless, creating a quality environment is the overall goal. "In the rush to solve our housing crisis we must not sacrifice design. We must not sacrifice quality," Oppenheimer says. What, then, is a quality environment? Goody suggests, "A good place to live in is indeed a living place: it has and it remembers its past, it is responsive to the needs of its present occupants, and it suggests that there will be future changes to come. Unlike the identical, sterile, 'faceless blocks' of the housing project (where the only changes are through defacement and graffati), a good place to live in has variety and invites personalizations. It may have a subtle variety—of differently shaped windows or roofs, of color for trim or doors, of garden fences or plantings. Ideally these variations and changes will have occurred over a long period of time, with each generation making its additions and alterations, enriching the whole."[4]

What makes for high-quality, low-cost housing

hinges on site, budget, regulatory contraints, whether the project is a renovation or new construction, the architect's skills, the program, and the management. As Donlyn Lyndon suggests, however, several universal elements help "make places that people can call home":

• Light is important because it makes everything else in a place come alive. Shifting patterns and tonalities that well-placed'light can give to a dwelling signal relationships to the immediate surroundings.

• Outlook, which is different from view. Outlook in dense housing is specific, filled with information about the collective of which it is a part, and crucial to the sense of differentiation that real places must develop. This requires the placement of openings that are specific to the dwelling and its position in the larger site. Stamped-out patterns won't work. Looking from inside to out and from outside to in is a form of social exchange that needs subtle modulation. Privacy should be attainable, not physically enforced. Suggestively defined outdoor spaces establish territories for sociable exchange.

• Movement contributes to the sense of underlying ease that is essential to feeling at home. The core movements in a place should be compact but gracious, not harshly channeled; this does not necessarily equate with an efficient core.

• Dignity lies in the allowance for making choices. Any housing community should include several forms of dwelling organization to allow for differences in living patterns and interests—even for differences in how we imagine ourselves. Good housing environments always go beyond what is simply expected. It is that extra care that counts: a craftsman's ingenuity in construction, a designed accommodation to existing features, or a tenant's investment in tulips. There must be space in which to improvise; niches and ledges and boundaries to collect the inhabitant's ongoing attention. Ideally the occupants will first have a hand, or at least a voice, in creating the place, so that it becomes their own even as it is being built.

The dialogue concerning appropriate housing for the homeless is not a decade old, yet already a substantial body of knowledge exists. Generally shelters fall into three categories— emergency, transitional, and long-term. In the ideal situation a homeless person would spend only a few days or weeks in an emergency shelter while adequate transitional housing is being found that offers the particular social services that individual needs. Transitional shelter can take a variety of forms but is usually more similiar to permanent housing than emergency shelter. The duration of stay obviously varies with each individual and each shelter, but typically the shortest duration is three months. More differentiation by population group occurs, with different groups (such as families, the chronically mentally ill, unemployed single adults, and children) being sent to different shelters. In this transitional phase more emphasis is placed on rehabilitation, both social and psychological. The ultimate goal is securing long-term housing. Emergency shelters tend to take the form of dormitories. Transitional and longer-term housing more closely follow traditional housing practices.

Most important for all three types is the creation of an environment that offers a sense of dignity to the guest, provides spaces for both privacy and socializing, has offices for or is located near social services, is domestic rather than institutional in ambience, and uses existing resources to the greatest extent possible without sacrificing design quality. Other design suggestions follow:

• Small shelters are preferable to large ones. Some shelter providers say that as many as 200 to 300 guests is manageable, a size others consider too large for any personal attention to be given.

• The environment should be welcoming, accessible, and undemanding.

• Adequate facilities should be provided for personal hygiene, as well as kitchen, infirmary, and laundry facilities.

• Adequate security is extremely important, particularly in shelters for women and children.

# LOW-COST HOUSING REDEFINED

• The homeless should be involved in deciding what the shelter should look like and how it should work.

• Easy maintenance is important.

• Natural light should be used whenever possible.

(For examples of how these and other objectives can be met, see the Search for Shelter case studies, pp. 12-87. For a concise list of general requirements for all three types of shelters, see the Chicago Search for Shelter, p. 32. For a more thorough examination of the design of shelters for the homeless see *The Search for Shelter*, the companion publication to this book.)

The line between housing for the homeless and low-cost housing is most blurred in shared housing, now emerging across the country as a legitimate housing type for certain populations—single men and women, the elderly, the chronically mentally ill, and single adults with children. Shared housing can run the gamut from single-room-occupancy hotels (previously known as residential hotels or flop houses)—where each resident has his or her own room but shares bathrooms, kitchens, and lounges—to a single-family house renovated into a group home.

"There's no question that SROs are a viable, acceptable form of housing accommodation," says Conrad Levenson, whose New York City firm specializes in low-cost housing. "It's not the accommodation of choice for everyone. But for single individuals who do not want or cannot accept the responsibility or the cost of a full, self-contained unit, or who otherwise might benefit from the shared housing experience, it's a very desirable housing type."

SROs vary significantly in size and arrangements, but certain design principles have been identified. An SRO for the chronically mentally ill, for example, may require 24-hour supervision and small communal spaces. SROs for single adults could more easily operate with larger lounges. Other ingredients for success are protected outdoor common areas, good in-house management, and in-house

social services or the proximity to such needed services. Quality design—attention to space, light, form, scale, and proportion—can have a tremendous impact.

Newly renovated SROs are highly valued by their occupants. In a newly renovated SRO for older adults in Brooklyn, none of the new residents showed up the first morning for breakfast in the communal dining room, relates Cindy Harden, director of the Pratt Architectural Center in New York City. Apparently the residents were so unaccustomed to having their own rooms—since most had previously been living in shelters or on the streets—that they did not want to venture out for fear that their rooms would be quickly taken from them.

In the 1970s the pioneers of SROs in San Francisco, New York City, Portland, Ore., and elsewhere faced tremendous obstacles in legitimizing residential hotels as a viable type. As development of office space boomed in the inner cities, so did the destruction of SROs. The demolition pace was so quick that New York City and San Francisco (and later other cities) enacted moratoriums on the destruction of SROs. By the early 1980s renewed interest in SROs gained momentum across the country, but more than half the country's supply of SRO units (some 1,116,000 units) had been lost—to demolition, urban renewal, abandonment, and arson.

Not until 1980, when Congress amended the Housing Act of 1936, did SRO occupants become eligible for federal housing assistance, and even then that assistance was contingent on each respective city documenting the need for SROs because other housing was not available for poverty-stricken individuals. With the first HUD grant for SRO renovations, the city of Portland, Ore., was able to rehabilitate 247 SRO units in a rundown section of the city for less than $2 million—an average of $7,500 per unit, or a mire fraction of the cost of providing units under traditional Section 8 programs. Renovation of Portland's Park Havilland Section 8 project in another section of town would have cost $40,000 for each unit.

Federal regulations are not the only impediment to the renovation of SROs and other forms of shared housing. In many cities—New York, Chicago, Boston, Los Angeles, San Francisco, Portland, and Seattle, among others—building codes have been rewritten to allow for SROs. Where no code exists, the process of renovating an SRO can be a tremendously slow and painstaking task. In Chicago, for example, "SRO properties had more restrictions than unfurnished apartments, which obviously increased the SRO costs," explains Eric Rubenstein, of the Single-Room Operators Association. "For example, the city wanted us to tear out perfectly good 21-inch sinks and install 24-inch sinks." To do so makes the project economically unfeasible.

In New York State one- and two-family buildings come under one code, while all other residential development falls under the multiple-family codes. "You have to meet the same standards in a three-family house as you would in a 100-unit high rise. That is inappropriate and does away with the economies of doing three- and four-family housing versus one- and two-family units," says Kathleen Dorgan, director of the Capitol Hill Improvement Albany Center Corporation, a community design center.

Building codes define what elements are necessary in a new or renovated building to protect the health, safety, and welfare of the occupants. Codes cover building structure, electrical systems, number of exits, and fire protection measures. Codes also call for a certain number of bathrooms and fixtures per building occupant, heating system efficiencies, proper food storage and cooking facilities, and minimum room size. Group homes are subject to codes that ensure accessibility to the handicapped; these cover such things as doors, elevators, bathrooms, kitchenettes, and turning radius to provide for wheelchair maneuvers.

Although in place to protect tenants' health and safety, local building codes can also add unnecessary expense and delay to the rehabilitation of low-cost housing, housing experts argue. Kate Lane, of the Chicago-based nonprofit organization Bethel New Life, recounts, "When we renovated low-cost housing, I had to fight for an exemption from placing a light bulb in a closet." The code discussion can get as specific as the precise number of electric outlets needed in each room. Costs associated with building code compliance can put the cost of housing—and particularly shelters for the homeless and long-term shared housing—beyond the reach of prospective tenants.

Confusion also can arise if a project has to comply with more than one building code. In Maryland, for example, deferred maintenance work costing $7,000 per unit for a group of rowhouses had to meet a city housing code, city rehabilitation standards, state rehabilitation standards, and state historic standards. Only through tough negotiation an additional cost of $4,000 was avoided. Uniform building standards for new construction and renovation could go a long way in easing these conflicts, some housing experts argue; the Building Officials and Code Administrators (BOCA) codes are thought to be capable of providing that uniformity.

Codes for SROs and other shared housing types in new markets have spurred heated debate about what the accepted standard of housing should be in this country. "We have developed a housing standard that is beyond the reach of affordable housing in any way, sharp, or form," Mary Comerio says. "We continue to make housing units that require, say, $700 a month rent for a two-bedroom unit to be profitable. So the federal government through Section 8 pays $600 of the rent and the tenant pays $100." To Comerio, this approach does not make sense economically.

In 1987 Comerio headed a team from Berkeley's Center for Environmental Change in investigating for the city of San Francisco the effect of seismic upgrading on low-income housing. The investigators found that most of the buildings in the city's Chinatown, Tenderloin, and Bush Street Corridor neighborhoods — traditionally low-income communities — were unreinforced brick, built between 1906 and 1925. Recent structural engineering advancements have led officials in some areas of the state to retrofit such buildings to meet a higher seismic safety standard. But often the cost of seimic upgrading is so high that owners simply demolish their buildings. A change in the San Francisco code could affect more than 25,000 units.

Comerio's team concluded that seismic upgrading of $5,000 to $10,000 would add $66 to $198 to the monthly rent of each unit, a steep increase for low-income residents. In addition, the team predicted, a significant number of buildings most likely would be torn down. "In essence," the team concluded, "anything but the minimal seismic upgrading would have a significant negative impact on building owners and tenants. . . . Changing the building code alone could cause more housing problems that it solves."

Space requirements are also being scrutinized. "We think of a minimum house as being 1,000 square feet," says Annette Anderson, of the East Tennessee Community Design Center and leader of the Knoxville Search for Shelter. "I think we'll start looking at a minimum house as 600 or 700 square feet as the best way to reduce the cost of construction. We'll have to increase things like shared space."

The effect of size on the affordability of housing is highly influenced by location. In San Francisco, for example, architect Donald MacDonald, FAIA, designed, developed, and marketed 10 infill projects with 57 single-family units. The units are tiny, ranging from about 600 to 900 square feet including garages; the offering prices have ranged from $115,000 to $165,000. Although they offer smaller than average and unconventionally arranged space, these units are intended for first-time homeowners of above-average means who want to live in close proximity to downtown. Newly constructed or renovated housing for people with low incomes is economically feasible only with massive subsidies — low-interest mortgages, tenant rent assistance or grants or low-interest loans from public and private groups for the purchase of land, construction costs, and building maintenance.

Through the "monopoly" houses in San Francisco, MacDonald proves that small may not be better but it can at least be comfortable. In a study to determine how to encourage families to reside in New York City's Battery Park mixed-use project, Goody, Clancy & Associates found that even luxury units were so small that there was hardly any way to reduce a typical unit's size to make it affordable. In fact, they found, families with children need even bigger ("eat in") kitchens and more storage than typically found. The only savings in the total construction costs (between 5 and 10 percent) could be realized in stripping down the luxury units — eliminating fancy finishes, top-of-the-line appliances, and expensive cabinetry.

Also in New York City, John Ellis & Associates Architects were commissioned by the New York Partnership to study cost effectiveness in the partnership's affordable housing projects specifically targeted to middle-income homeownership. The comparison of 10 projects found significant cost differences resulting from minor differences in code requirements, structural systems, and site conditions. One of the most dramatic findings was the cost-effectiveness of light-weight, low-rise housing. "Specifically, usable space may cost over twice as much in a high-rise as it does in three-story, two-family housing. Put another way, the same amount of money would build 80 to 100 equal size units of low-rise housing. This is a much greater cost difference than most housing professionals are aware of. The potential housing policy aspects of this are intriguing, to say the least," concludes John M. Ellis, AIA.

The Ellis study made other important findings:
• All-wood construction was the least expensive,

followed closely by noncombustible wood exterior walls; steel frame; masonry load-bearing walls and wood joists; steel frame and truss; and masonry bearing walls and concrete plank.

• The three modular units were lower priced but also were of lower quality in terms of livability, appearance, workmanship, and the neighborhood they created. . . . "The modulars could and should make excellent, economical housing," the study concluded.

• "The evidence of the very limited sample of this study suggests that one- and two-family houses can be built more economically than three-family, and that all three of these types may be more economical than multiple dwellings."

• "Foundation costs vary widely (from $5,000 to $16,000/DU). In addition, a variety of systems have been used on these projects, including wood piles, steel piles, and spread footings. No one of them is the 'best' or the most cost-effective system. Different foundation systems are recommended for different social conditions."

• Recurring problems surrounded subsurface conditions, which "caused more delays and unanticipated costs than any other conditions. . . . Better, more rigorous soil testing and subsurface analysis is necessary, leading to more thorough foundation design."

In conclusion, the Ellis group suggests that the "two- and three-story wood frame, site-built or steel frame, modular one- and two-family construction is two to three times more cost effective than multi-story, fire resistive, multiple dwelling construction." The light-weight construction is favored because of its "greater efficiency of use of space, lower construction cost per square foot, lower soft cost due to greater standardization and simpler logistics."

A cost-cutting method for the rehabilitation of low-cost housing has been widely tested by the Enterprise Foundation, a nonprofit community development orgranization founded by Columbia, Md., developer James Rouse. With financial backing largely from Rouse's festival marketplaces, the

foundation works with nonprofit groups to reduce the cost of rehabilitation and new construction and financing. It also assists local organizations in providing housing management and delivering social and employment services. The network consists of 70 nonprofit groups in 27 cities.

In 1983 the Enterprise Foundation formed the Rehab Work Group comprised of community groups, architects, builders, and landlords that created, with imput from around the country, *The Cost Cuts Manual: Nailing Down Savings for Least-Cost Housing.* The manual focuses primarily on cutting construction costs—only part of the affordable housing picture, the group maintains, along with acquisi-

131

tion, financing, and operating costs. The approach stresses life-cycle cost—comparing options by weighing the cost of an improvement over its potential lifetime. The group acknowledges "there is no single magic trick to construction cost cutting. The state of the art of cost cutting is a myraid of little tricks and ideas each aimed at a small part of a home. . . . Necessity is the mother of invention, and the challenge of the loss of Federal funding becomes the opportunity to break loose from pre-conceptions about $50,000 per unit renovations."[6] The Rehab Work Group has developed a compendium of cost-saving techniques:
• Given a choice, do not select badly dilapidated properties.
• Rehabilitate occupied rather than vacant properties.
• Work specifications should be done by the agency doing the rehabilitation.
• Undertake "partial" rather than "gut" rehabilitation to save as many of the existing systems as possible.
• Choose repair methods and materials carefully.
• Downsize rather than upsize—i.e. do not rehabilitate more space than the tenant needs.
• Reconfigure floor plans as little as possible.
• Apply prudent rehabilitation codes rather than new construction ones.
• Work with tenants or owners in the units to be rehabilitated, thus avoiding relocation.
• On smaller jobs use neighborhood tradespeople or in-house crews.
• Use salvaged or bargain-priced materials.
• Work on several small projects rather than a single large one.

A great deal of emphasis is placed on partial rehabilitation. "If it ain't broke, don't fix it" is the Rehab Work Group's motto. "Successful low-cost renovations mean fixing what is fixable, replacing what is broken, and adding only what is necessary to reduce costs for energy, maintenance, and operation. Successful low-cost renovations mean not blindly replacing everything in sight, but rather, analyzing each component of the building to find needed repairs for a continuing useful life. Patching and painting an old wall is a lot less expensive and time-consuming than tearing down the wall and building a new one. Even the oldest buildings often have some modern wiring. Adding new outlets and circuits usually costs less than replacing the entire electrical system."[7]

Should modern codes and standards be redefined, given today's housing crisis? *The Cost Cuts Manual* advocates, "Don't change floor plans. . . . A housing group in Colorado received a design from its architect calling for extensive demolition and rearrangement of partitions. The reason? Tenants had to walk through their single bedroom to get to the kitchen—a modern no no. Yet, the elderly tenants—singles and couples—had no need or desire for the privacy that would cost $2,500 per apartment."

To the Rehab Work Group every expense is suspect. This includes architects' and engineers' fees and labor costs. While not advocating the elimination of architects and engineers from the design and development of low-cost housing, the rehab work group does suggest that community development groups educate themselves as to when the expertise of architects and engineers is crucial and when it is not. More damaging, however, can be the labor costs. The federal Davis-Bacon law requires workers to be paid the prevailing wage set by the U.S. Department of Labor for specific geographic regions if the project is federally funded. This law can raise total job costs from zero to 50 percent above comparable nonfederal and nonunion jobs.

Ways to diminish Davis-Bacon labor costs include making the purchase of a building contingent on a list of specific repairs that the owner will make before the sale. The Davis-Bacon Act will not influence labor costs for those improvements. If the project must comply with Davis-Bacon wage scales, the Rehab Work Group suggests pushing the project to completion quickly.

A way to reduce building costs is for tenants, owners, or volunteers to partially or totally construct or renovate housing themselves. Some 20 percent of all single-family houses built annually involve some degree of self-help, the Enterprise Foundation's Rehab Work Group maintains. Savings can be substantial. According to the February 1981 issue of *New Shelter* magazine, 20 percent of the cost of a new home can be saved if an owner takes on the contractor role. If an owner finishes the interior of a contractor-built shell, savings can reach 44 percent. If the house is entirely built by the owner, the cost can be reduced 58 percent, and if recycled building materials are used, the cost can be reduced by 65 to 72 precent.

"Self-help housing may be the only way for low-income people to afford to own a decent home," the Rehab Work Group says. But there are other benefits: "Because people have a personal investment in their home, they develop strong feelings of ownership and responsibility. Through self-help labor, people learn skills and develop attitudes that can assist them in maintaining their home over the years. In multi-family housing, self-help work can enhance the success of property management and maintenance. In the case of resident self-management, the improvement can mean the difference between success and failure."

Michael J. Crosbie, senior editor of *Architecture* and of the Essex, Conn., firm Centerbrook Architects, wrote in 1983 that the involvement of millions of people springs from "the need to extend one's self and the reflection of one's world into the place of habitation. The home becomes the respository of values and beliefs, and through the dwellers' active involvement it is the physical evidence of their creative energy. It not only reflects what is meaningful to the builders, but because of the fact that it exists through their efforts it in turn makes their action meaningful. It is an affirmation that their lives have meaning and purpose. It is for these reasons that the homes of owner-builders are worthy of the designation 'architecture': the art of building."

Neither Crosbie nor the Rehab Work Group suggest that self-helpers do the entire task. For low-income housing, the Rehab Work Group calls for an "experienced construction supervisor who writes up the work, lays it out, orders materials, and schedules workers and contractors. The supervisor also checks the quality of work and trains people to do the work."

There are several ways to appoarch self-help housing. The U.S. Farmers Home Administration, for instance, offers grants for a construction supervisor, land acquisition, and construction financing at very low interest for self-help projects in rural areas. Financing starting at one percent is offered. Housing is usually constructed by mutual self-help groups. Units usually range from $2,500 to $10,000 per piece.

In partial self-help projects a contractor takes a much stronger leadership role, setting the pace of construction. In New York City members of the Urban Homesteading Assistance Board participate in partial self-help programs. For a $30,000 to $35,000 unit, the city will offset costs with a $15,000-per-unit, one percent loan over 30 years.

Perhaps the most widely known self-help program today is Habitat of Humanity, which basically consists of volunteers and future homeowners together building low-cost housing. Based in Americus, Ga., Habitat for Humanity is an international network of local church-based groups, with more than 240 affiliates in the U.S. The goal is to build single-family houses, which are sold at no profit and for which homeowners pay no interest on loans. The volunteers come from the local Habitat core groups and one-time and staff volunteers. One to 20 houses per year are built at each affiliate's location.

Clearly the need to find new ways of reducing the cost of housing will continue well into the 1990s. Will there be any breakthroughs in building technology that could lower costs? Perhaps most crucial will be determining whether cost reduction adversely affects housing standards in this country. Just as important, though, will be the debate over what role the federal government should take with regards to an affordable housing crisis that continues to expand.

# A COMMITMENT
# TO CARING

Unless drastic steps are taken soon, prognosticators warn, the 1990s can bring only a broadening of the affordable housing crisis. And as the search for solutions continues, the nation must first determine whether the four-decade-old commitment to decent housing and a suitable environment for all Americans should be renewed. How will that commitment be met in this era of soaring federal budget deficits and rising housing costs? What should America's national housing policy be?

A chilling prediction comes from Phillip L. Clay, a professor at the Massachusetts Institute of Technology. Extrapolating from current housing trends for the Neighborhood Reinvestment Corporation, Clay concluded that by the year 2003 the gap between "the total low-rent housing supply (subsidized and unsubsidized) and households needing such housing is projected to grow to 7.8 million units." Depending on average household size, this gap could represent some 18 million Americans—people who would ultimately move in with family or friends or into substandard housing, pay a disproportionate share of their already modest incomes for housing, or sink into homelessness.

Already there is evidence of doubling up. The New York City Housing Authority, for example, estimated in 1983 that some 17,000 families were illegally doubled up in its 150,000 units. The problem was described as growing geometrically."[1]

That same year the U.S. Census Bureau recorded 7 million households living in "overcrowded" conditions (more than one person per room); 700,000 were living in conditions described as "extremely overcrowded" (1.5 people per room).

Being forced out of overcrowded housing conditions often results in homelessness. "Being homeless is now recognized as the end product of a rental housing supply that is increasingly inadequate in terms of volume, condition, unit sizes, and rent levels," maintains housing expert Mary K. Nenno. For the homeless, shelters have taken the place of rental housing; the homeless can exist from day to day without the prospect of a better tomorrow.

This dead-end spiral has been well documented. Helpers of the homeless—individuals, nonprofit organizations, and local and state governments—find themselves in a Catch-22 situation: While aiming to provide the best possible shelter and services for the homeless, are we institutionalizing the state of homelessness? Are shelters for the homeless becoming modern-day almshouses? Shouldn't resources be directed soley to creating permanent housing and long-term rehabilitative services? Yet, if that happens where can the homeless find refuge?

For architects and providers of shelters the inclination to provide comfortable surroundings is admirable. Yet in the process, is a much lower standard of living becoming acceptable for the most destitute among us? And, again, shouldn't resources be directed toward long-term, low-cost housing.

One example: The Community for Creative Non-Violence, an advocacy group for the homeless headed by Mitch Synder, fought long and hard to gain from the federal government a building in Washington, D.C., and money for its renovation into a shelter for the homeless. Before renovation the building was unfit for human habitation, yet as many as 1,000 people found shelter there, according to CCNV. Inside that building the smell of urine was overwhelming. The halls were a dingy institutional green, doors and windows were broken, holes were punched in the plaster wall, bathrooms were inadequate and filthy. Yet, this was the permanent home for many; some even attempted to create a homey atmosphere around their cots.

In dramatic fashion CCNV won possession of the building located a half mile from the Capitol: Snyder went on a hunger fast to force the federal government to capitulate. On the eve of a "60 Minutes" broadcast on the CCNV fight, President Reagan, on board Air Force One, gave in: Snyder would have his renovated shelter.

To aid in its design, five advanced architecture students from the City College in New York set up shop inside the building. Architects, interior designers, and others refined the students' scheme.

Opened in October 1988 the CCNV shelter is in a gleaming, renovated building. Designed for 1,000 men and women, the capacity has been raised to 1,700. The design brought light, cleanliness, and adequate bathroom and kitchen facilities. And by separating the building into five "mini" shelters, it also brought a more comprehendable unit population. It now seems workable when partially full, yet the living conditions are far below the national standard. Some will live here a year or two, maybe three. It might be a different atmosphere altogether when full.

"Shelters are inappropriate substitutes for long-term housing, and attempts to respond to immediate needs can deflect energy and resources from longer-term initiatives.... Yet, the problem of homelessness will persist and grow in the U.S. until the diminution and deterioration of housing units for people with low-income are reversed and affordable housing is made more widely available," concluded a 13-member panel of experts examining homelessness, health, and human needs for the National Academy of Sciences.

The quality of services to the homeless—health care, job and housing placement, counseling—are also suspect. As with shelter, the lack of funding is evident: When the CCNV shelter opened, one volunteer psychiatrist was lined up for one night a week to work with shelter residents—a ratio of 1,000 to one.

"Adequate services must be provided, but without permanently institutionalizing homeless families and individuals through another human service system that inherently provides second-class services," concluded the National Academy of Sciences panel. The panel closely links services to housing, but gives priority to housing. "More than anything else, homeless people need stable residences.... Decent housing is not only socially desirable but is necessary for the prevention of disease and the promotion of health," the panel contends.

Currently an additional 5.5 million low-income units are needed, estimates the National Alliance to End Homelessness, a group of housing experts from private, public, and nonprofit organizations working in the low-income housing arena. "Clearly, homelessness and a lack of affordable housing have reached crisis proportions in this nation. Without a strong, direct federal commitment, we will simply be unable to deal effectively with the roots of the homelessness problem. The long-term social and economic impact to all Americans will be devastating," says Alliance Chairman Clifford L. Alexander Jr. And although states and local governments are playing larger roles in providing that low-cost housing, "supply issues need to be addressed at the national level," the Alliance maintains.

Existing low-cost housing needs to be preserved. "The stock of affordable housing in place," Phillip Clay says, "would cost more than a quarter of a trillion dollars to replace for the target population that continues to grow. Yet, we face for the rest of this century and into the next, the possibility of losing a majority of these units in an economic and financial environment in which this housing would not be replaced either by public action or by the private market." That battle is being lost every day. From 1973 to 1983, 4.5 million units were permanently removed from the nation's housing stock either by demolition or conversion for commercial use; approximately half of those units had been occupied by low-income households.

The decline of low-cost housing in this country is intricately tied to federal housing policy. Beginning with the 1938 Housing Act, the federal government has been the primary source of direct subsidies for the construction and maintenance of low-income housing. Over the years the number of these units has increased steadily, peaking at 300,000 units added annually in the 1970s.

In the early 1980s the emphasis changed rather drastically from large federal subsidies for low-income housing production to rent subsidies for landlords and eventually rent vouchers for tenants. At the same time, available low-cost housing grew scarcer, because of urban renewal, abandonment, demolition, and upgrading in hot markets. Looming in the near future is the expiration of five- and 15-year contracts between the federal government and private owners of subsidized housing. The U.S. General Accounting Office estimates that as many as 900,000 units could be lost by the turn of the century. This alone could cause significant increases in the number homeless. In addition, the nation's investment in public housing has not been adequately maintained. HUD reported in 1987 that $25 billion was needed for repairs; many units are simply being abandoned.

By the end of the deficit-ridden 1980s, federal support for housing has been reduced by 60 percent. Federal support of the construction of new low-income housing has essentially disappeared. Low-cost housing is so scarce in parts of the country that 50 percent of those eligible for low-cost housing are not able to find any.

In the private market, the gentrification of urban neighborhoods continues. While urban renewal and renovation have been applauded in deteriorating neighborhoods, the casualties of that redevelopment—people living in low-cost housing—are often ignored. Their only option often is an environment of even greater squalor—or the streets.

The private development market has virtually stopped contributing to the low-income housing stock as federal subsidies and tax benefits have dried up. In today's market a private developer cannot make a profit producing housing that low-income persons can afford. *The New Republic* economics writer Robert Kuttner provides useful data: "It costs a certain irreducible minimum to keep a dwelling in decent repair and pay the utility bills and local taxes. Even an apartment with a market value of zero still costs about $300 a month to operate, which is beyond the means of somebody earning the miminum wage."

As the 1980s have progressed, more often than not the only option in housing has been "trickle down" rather than "trickle up." Even prospective first-time, middle-income home buyers are affected. As a consequence, homeownership among the middle class is declining for the first time since World War II.

"In the 1980s housing has become the great divider of the haves and have-nots," Kuttner maintains. "A have is somebody who owns his own house, and effortlessly increases his net worth as the value of the house inflates. A have-not is a tenant of moderate means, vulnerable to a shrinking supply of rental housing, the threat of condo conversion, and steadily escalating rent costs. Homelessness is only the most graphic emblem of a drastic shortage of affordable housing. The shortage of affordable housing reflects the simple fact that poor people don't make enough money to buy decent shelter at a price that the market can economically provide." This is where the federal government or some other benevolent entity needs to step in. In the 1990s the cost, however, may be prohibitively expensive.

"The federal government is progressively withdrawing from financial responsibility for the deep needs in our cities, and there seems to be widespread support for such withdrawal," says James Rouse, the Columbia, Md., developer whose Enterprise Foundation gives financial and technical assistance to nonprofit housing organizations. "People are disenchanted with big government programs, which are seen as bureaucratic, too costly, ineffective, building dependence, and sapping creativity and initiative.... This judgment may be rationalized but it simply says that the basic systems of our society are in serious disrepair. The needs of the people in our cities are real and mounting. Conditions are clear—increasing homelessness, poverty, growing pools of unemployment, drugs, crime."[2]

As the federal government has pulled away from low-cost housing, state and local governments and nonprofit organizations have attempted to take over. Although their resources are limited and can never totally replace the federal government's, their creativity to put together shelter for the homeless and low-cost housing seems boundless. Modest ways to involve the public sector in the delivery of low-cost housing have been discovered. But in the end, most housing experts agree, our national housing ills can be solved only through a new federal commitment to do just that.

Work on the creation of a new national housing policy is already underway. To be introduced in Congress in 1989, when the next President and Administration in place, legislation is being developed under the sponsorship of Senators Alan Cranston (D.-Calif.) and Alfonse M. D'Amato (R.-N.Y.), respectively, the 100th Congress's chairman and ranking minority member of the Senate subcommittee on housing and urban affairs during the 100th Congress. Provisions of that housing legislation will draw from recommendations of the National Housing Task Force established in September 1987 as part of that Congressional effort to re-examine American's housing policy. It was comprised of 26 individuals of diverse experience in housing policy, production, and finance; it was chaired by James Rouse and vice-chaired by David O. Maxwell, chairman and chief executive officer of the Federal National Mortgage Association.

In its published report *A Decent Place to Live*, the National Housing Task Force called for a bipartisan effort on the part of federal, state, and local concerns to provide decent housing opportunities for all Americans by the year 2000. "A decent place for a family to live becomes a platform for dignity and self-respect and a base for hope and improvement. A decent home allows people to take advantage of opportunities in education, health, and employment—the means to get ahead in our society. A decent home is the important beginning point for growth into the mainstream of American life," concluded the task force (known also as the Rouse-Maxwell task force).

The National Housing Task Force recommended a "series of concrete actions. . . . First must be a commitment from the federal government to shape the national housing agenda. . . . We would not have

come as far as we have in meeting our housing needs if the federal government had not exercised this responsibility in the past. . . . The simple device of pledging the full faith and credit of the federal government revolutionized the nation's housing system by making possible long-term mortgages at a fixed cost with low down payments—turning America into a nation of homeowners." Now, a new "revolution" is needed to ensure an adequate supply of low-cost housing by the turn of the century.

The centerpiece of the task force's recommendations is the creation of a Housing Opportunity Program (HOP), which would provide federal funds to local, state, and nonprofit organizations to create low-cost housing. In turn those organizations would be required to raise matching funds from public and private sources, see housing projects through completion, and in many cases oversee maintenance and operation. The HOP funds would be provided with "maximum flexibility and minimum regulation." The first-year goal would be to build, renovate, repair, or acquire 150,000 to 200,000 units nationwide.

To provide new sources of capital for the development of low-cost housing, the Rouse-Maxwell task force recommended that the federal government participate in benevolent lending programs. Through such programs individuals, corporations, churches, foundations, and other groups are encouraged to lend funds at rates as low as 3 percent to finance low-income housing.

Securing capital in this way has already proved successful: Jubilee Housing, a nonprofit neighborhood housing corporation in Washington, D.C., has raised more than $2 million from 400 lenders at an average rate of 2.5 percent. The Institute for Community Economics has received $4.5 million in deposits for its national revolving loan fund and has financed more than 25 community projects, the majority of which are housing projects. Federal deposit insurance of these loans would reduce the risk involved, the Rouse-Maxwell task force maintains, which in turn could greatly increase the volume of deposits. In addition, the federal government should promote community development banks, which would function in much the same way as the financial institutions mentioned above.

According to the task force, emphasis should also be placed on the renovation of existing buildings, the preservation of privately owned, federally assisted housing, and the restoration of public housing, with the worst housing projects targeted for immediate attention. Tenants should be encouraged to become involved in management, the task force recommended, and federal tax benefits should be used to support low-income housing. An additional 100,000 units of rental assistance over and above the administration's requirements for fiscal year 1989 should be approved by Congress.

"There is clearly a broad consensus among housing experts on the national housing crisis, and new, promising approaches for addressing it. What's needed now is some serious money," Robert Kuttner writes. While considered a large amount of money in the Gramm-Rudman budget cutting era, the $3 billion, first-year addition to the HUD budget recommended by the Rouse-Maxwell task force is considered modest compared to the nation's housing ills.

Federal outlays for HUD programs in 1989 are expected to be $13.6 billion. An increase of $3 billion would represent less than a 25 percent increase in total expenditures for HUD housing programs. The National Housing Institute, by comparison, reported in 1988 that to stem the rising tide of homelessness 7.5 million new low-income housing units will be needed by the year 2000—at a cost of $300 billion.

To gain more perspective on these potential costs, the quantity of indirect housing "subsidies" that middle- and high-income people receive must be acknowledged; through the mortgage interest deduction the federal government spends about four times as much—a total of $38.8 billion in fiscal year 1987—on middle- and upper-class housing as on housing subsidies for the poor. While it

is unlikely that any changes will be made soon in these deductions, low-income housing advocates will continue to lobby to redirect part of the money to low-income housing. A 1988 Congressional Budget Office report estimated that nearly $10 billion could be raised in the next five years by capping the mortgage interest deduction at $12,000 for an individual's tax return or $20,000 for a joint return. Less than one-half of one percent of all taxpayers would be affected.

Clearly any changes in federal housing policy will be the subject of much debate in Congress, with rebuttals to the Rouse-Maxwell recommendations from other organizations and experts in the field. Meanwhile some trends are emerging: Local nonprofit groups continue to grow in sophistication and play an increasingly larger role in the delivery of low-cost housing, with varied sources of revenues; new or little used ways to provide low-cost housing for perpetuity are gaining ground, such as the mutual housing concept; and low-cost housing is becoming more closely linked with social services that can help prevent homelessness—health care, job training, life management skills, foreclosure prevention, among others.

Since the early 1960s community-based development corporations have formed to aid in the housing and community development, particularly in neighborhoods suffering from disinvestment. (These CDCs should not be confused with community design centers, mentioned in chapter three). Now community development corporations (CDCs) can be found in nearly every state; in the mid-1980s there were an estimated 1,000 CDCs, of varying sizes and accomplishments and even different names ("neighborhood development organizations" is one such deviation). They have served as developer of housing and financier and operator of shopping centers, industrial parks, and retail shops. In the last decade CDCs have grown into sophisticated engines of change in neighborhoods more accustomed to decay rather than rebirth. CDCs draw on local and state government resources and the aid of private nonprofit founda- 139 tions. Neighborhood Reinvestment circulates $100 million through a revolving loan to its Neighborhood Housing Services.

"This movement, largely invisible to the society at large, is quintessentially American. It mirrors the qualities of our society that so impressed Alexis de Tocqueville in the 1830s; our penchant for innovative civic association, our belief that individuals can bring about change, our openness to risk taking and to bridging lines of class, ideology, and party. CDCs, in their quiet way, have become a major component of corrective capitalism; in this free-enterprise nation they are finding ways to open doors to classes and individuals otherwise excluded from the American Dream."[3]

The CDC movement is one that changes with the times, scurrying to find needed capital for much needed community projects. "Many of today's CDCs are becoming adept at hooking into the 1980s culture of small business, entrepreneurial growth, and building a capacity for indigenous economic development in communities long plagued by poverty and dependency," say urbanologists Neal Peirce and Carol Steinbach. "One need only take changes in prevailing CDC strategies for generating jobs. During the 1960s and 1970s, CDCs focused largely on trying to start their own businesses. Many failed. Today's CDCs, by contrast, are more likely to supply equity capital, loans, incubator space, and technical assistance in support of home-grown private entrepreneurs and businesses in their midst.[4]

Take the Marshall Heights Community Development Organization, Inc. (MHCDO), as an example. In the summer of 1988 the formal opening of a new Safeway grocery in a struggling neighborhood in Washington, D.C., was considered a substantial victory. Besides convincing Safeway to be an anchor in that small neighborhood shopping center (where in the past disinvestment was much more common), MHCDO recruited employees for the store. MHDCO has been a moving force in the city's Ward 7 for the last decade. It is active in the development of housing, business, human (education, training, and employ-

ment), infrastructure, and organizational resources. In 1988 it began to seek transitional and permanent housing for families with employed head(s) of households.

More than most organizations, community development corporations have been in touch with neighborhood housing needs. Looking to such groups to provide guidance in developing and carrying out national housing policies should ultimately lead to more livable and humane environments that meet the needs of the residents. The same can be said of community design organizations. "The first principle of community design is to recognize the rights of all citizens to have a voice in decisions that affect the places they inhabit, work, and linger," says Mary Comerio, an architect in the San Francisco Bay Area who specializes in community design. "The design of housing and public places should involve the rational and poetic understanding of what makes a place work and what makes it special and significant," she concludes.

New ways of offering long-term, low-cost housing is being investigated. "We should search for new ideas that move us closer to the ideal scheme for housing the poor—a scheme that is not tied to larger investment trends, is affordable in perpetuity, is capable of self-expansion and regeneration, is owned by an entity that has an interest in maintaining a high quality of life, and which is supportive of resident pride," M.I.T.'s Phillip Clay says. A model program is West Germany's mutual housing system; comprised of 15 million housing units built since World War II. Under the Neighborhood Reinvestment model the mutual housing association is a combination of title and tenure. As a corporate entity it owns the property, renting units to its members. Each member pays a capital fee to qualify for a unit (about 5 percent of the unit's value); the fee is returned with nominal interest when the member moves. Although members do not participate in long-term capital investment, they enjoy a voice in management and the security of long-term tenure. Currently there are 1,000 such units in the United States.

Mutual housing in this country will not appeal to all income groups. Middle- and upper-income groups will more likely pursue homeownership, and people in the very-low-income strata will not be able to afford the minimum monthly payment needed to cover operating, maintenance, and replacement costs (between $265 and $380 per month plus utilities). Mutual housing associations can be quite effect in a neighborhood that is in the process of disinvestment; here the magnitude of an association's housing rehabilition may assure residents that, indeed, the neighborhood will be a good place to live. Mutual housing development can also work to keep residents from being displaced in gentrifying neighborhoods.

As with the community-based development corporations, the emphasis is on creating decent homes in decent neighborhoods. Of mutual housing, columnist Neal R. Peirce says, "This is not just bricks and mortar; it's a social bond, it's mutual cooperation; it's truly a home building partnership based on protection of precious housing resources by resourceful management." Each mutual housing association develops, owns, and manages its property. Members of a mutual housing association are residents, government and business representatives, and professional in real estate development and housing management.

A highly successful mutual housing project in this country is Alameda Place in Baltimore, which grew out of the successful track record of the Neighborhood Housing Services of Baltimore (part of Neighborhood Reinvestment's NeighborWorks network, which besides other activities aids in the establishment of mutual housing associations). Alameda consists of 110 new townhouses built on a once vacant, 10-acre site in older section of northeast Baltimore.

The Alameda Place mutual housing association's members "feel a sense of security about their future, as well as a sense of ownership in both their homes and the association itself, viewing it as a 'step up from rental,'" William A. Whiteside, executive direc-

© Maureen Fennelli

tor of Neighborhood Reinvestment, reported in 1985.

For the homeless the provision of affordable, permanent housing is the first step in that homeless person's reintegration into the community. "A decent place for a family to live becomes a platform for dignity and self-respect and a base for help and improvement. A decent home allows people to take advantage of opportunities in education, health, and employment—the means to get ahead of our society. A decent home is the important beginning point for growth into the mainstream of American life," maintains the National Housing Task Force.

But more and more, connecting that housing with community support services is seen as crucial. The National Academy of Science panel cautioned, "The homeless need the kind of social support systems and appropriate health care that would allow them to maintain themselves in the community. . . . With the proper support systems, many will outgrow their need for therapeutic milieus and specialized housing and will eventually become self-reliant. For some, however, the need may be lifelong."

The victims of homelessness aren't just the stereotypical "bums" anymore or the poorest of the poor; the crisis has reached working people and families, even those once considered securely positioned in the middle class. The statistics—and the reality—are shocking. In its annual survey of hunger and homelessness in 26 American cities, the U.S. Con-

141

# A COMMITMENT TO CARING

ference of Mayors found in 1987 that one-third of all homeless in those cities were families with young children—young children whose lives could be forever scarred by the traumas of homelessness.

If statistics don't make you a believer in the severity of the crisis, just look around you. Maybe that homeless man or woman you pass on the way to work each day will seem more like a lost soul than a threat. Or maybe when driving through a crumbling urban neighborhood you might wonder under what conditions live the children you see playing in the rubble of vacant lots. How precarious is their family's situation? To witness the most dreadful scene, just visit the public emergency shelters in any large city. It can be a horrifying journey into a world that more closely resembles a prison camp than a safe and warm haven. In the end, the ingredient needed most to heal the nation's housing ills is a commitment to caring.

Developer James Rouse asks. "The people of this country, the leaders of our business corporations, the managers of our wealth, do not know how the millions and millions of people in this country live. They may have read some figures or seen pictures of derelict neighborhoods, but they have not walked those streets. They have not climbed the stairs in those apartments, seen people living in that miserable housing, paying outrageous rents, frightened, hopeless, feeling abandoned by the society of which they are a part."

When one senses the inequities, when one begins to care, then the protests can begin. That, too, is an individual process. Ten of those 13 members of the National Academy of Sciences panel announced, in protest, that while they endorsed the findings of their panel, the final report "failed to capture our sense of shame and anger" about homelessness in this country. "Contemporary American homelessness is an outrage, a national scandal," the protesters said. "Its character requires a careful, sophisticated, and dispassionate analysis—which this report provides— but its tragedy demands something more direct and human, less qualified and detached. We have tried to present the facts and figures of homelessness, but we were unable to capture the extent of our anger and dismay. We have summarized available studies on homeless children, but we had no means to paint the pathos and tragedy of these displaced, damaged, innocent lives. We have reviewed the demographic and clinical data and then, walking home, passed men asleep on heating grates or displaced people energetically searching in garbage piles for a few cents' income from aluminum cans. We analyzed mortality data for the homeless but lacked any platform from which to shout that our neighbors are dying needlessly because we are incapable of providing the most basic services."

The commitment to caring can take a plethora of forms. It can be Maureen O'Connor, the mayor of San Diego, living on the streets and shelters for 48 hours, experiencing the crisis first hand. It can be the Mad Housers in Atlanta, professionals who on the weekend build shacks for the homeless as a message to city officials that someone cares if the homeless have a place to call home. It can be the participants of the Search for Shelter that volunteered a day's, a week's, or a month's work to help in the design of a shelter for the homeless.

Or the caring can be less direct: a vote for a candidate that offers some compassion, if not solutions, to local housing ills. Or maybe it's a court decision that will have lasting effect, like the 1988 decision in Yonkers, N.Y., where under severe punishment from the courts the city finally voted to approve a court-ordered desegregation housing plan. Or it can be when a wealthy community, like Hilton Head, N.C., decides that it needs to build low-income housing in its city so people with low-paying jobs in that resort town don't have to travel hours to work.

More than ever, people are begining to acknowledge the inequities that exist. The opportunity for all to have decent housing has a direct bearing on the greater well being of this nation. Still, there is so much left to be done, and in the end one wonders why so many others don't also see the need to care.

# NOTES

## NO PLACE TO CALL HOME

[1]*Housing the Homeless*, p. 3.

[2]Whitman, David. "Who's Who Among the Homeless," *The New Republic*, June 6, 1988, p. 18.

[3]*Homelessness: Critical Issues for Policy and Practice*, p. 22.

[4]*Housing the Homeless*, p. 3.

[5]*Homelessness: Critical Issues for Policy and Practice*, p. 22.

[6]Baxter, Ellen, and Kim Hopper. "Shelter and Housing for the Homeless Mentally Ill." *The Homeless Mentally Ill*. Richard H. Lamb, Ed. Washington, D.C. The American Psychiatric Association, 1984, p. 125-126.

[7]*Housing the Homeless*, p. 8.

[8]*The Search for Shelter*, p.34.

## PARTNERSHIPS FOR HOUSING

[1]*Homelessness: Critical Issues for Policy and Practice*, p. 11.

[2]*Housing the Homeless*, p. 313.

[3]*Community Relations Strategies: A Handbook for Sponsors of Community-Based Programs for the Homeless*, p. 13.

[4]*Inclusionary Housing Programs: Politics and Practices*, p. 11.

[5]*Ibid*, p. 1.

[6]*Nonfederal Housing Programs: How States and Localities Are Responding to Federal Cutbacks in Low-Income Housing*, p. 5.

[7]*Ibid*, p. 59.

[8]*At Risk of Loss: The Endangered Future of Low-Income Rental Housing Resources*, p. 24.

[9]*Ibid*, p. 25.

[10]*Nonfederal Housing Programs: How States and Localities Are Responding to Federal Cutbacks in Low-Income Housing*, p. 29.

[11]*Ibid*, p. 3.

## THE SEARCH FOR SHELTER

[1]Marcuse, Peter. "Criticism or Cooptation: Can Architects Reveal the Sources of Homelessness?" *CRIT*. Washington, D.C.: The American Institute of Architecture Students, v. 20, Spring 1988, p. 32.

## LOW-COST HOUSING REDEFINED

[1]Marcuse, p. 32.

[2]Braybrooke, Susan. "Two Old Hands Talk About Housing," *Architectural Record*. New York City, Feb. 1988, p. 122.

[3]Lyndon, Donlyn. "Essay on Social Housing," *Progressive Architecture*. Stamford, Conn., July 1984, p. 87.

[4]Goody, Joan, and John Clancy. "Essay on Social Housing," *Progressive Architecture*. Stamford, Conn., July 1984, p. 87.

[5]*Ibid*, p. 87.

[6]*The Cost Cuts Manual*, p. xii.

[7]*Ibid*, p. 3-1.

## A COMMITMENT TO CARING

[1]*Homelessness, Health, and Human Needs*, p. 26.

[2]*The Cost Cuts Manual*, p. ix.

[3]*Creative Capitalism: The Rise of America's Community Development Corporations*, p. 9.

[4]*Ibid*, p. 31.

# BIBLIOGRAPHY

Anello, Rose, and Tillie Shuster. *Community Relations Strategies: A Handbook for Sponsors of Community-Based Programs for the Homeless.* New York City: Community Service Society of New York, 1985.

*Building Affordable Housing: A Cost Savings Guide for Builder/Developers.* Washington, D.C.: NAHB Research Foundation, Inc., and U.S. Department of Housing and Urban Development, Office of Policy Development and Research.

Cassidy, Cecilia, Robert M. Santucci, Jim Thomas, and Peter Werwath. *The Cost Cuts Manual: Nailing Down Savings for Least-Cost Housing.* Columbia, Md.: The Enterprise Foundation, 1987.

Church, William, Sam Galbreath, and Andy Raubeson. *Single Room Occupancy Development Handbook.* Portland, Ore., and Los Angeles: Portland Development Corporation and SRO Housing Corporation, April 1985.

Clay, Phillip L. *At Risk of Loss: The Endangered Future of Low-Income Rental Housing Resources.* Washington, D.C.: Neighborhood Reinvestment Corporation, 1987.

Committee on Health Care for Homeless People, Institute of Medicine. *Homelessness, Health and Human Needs.* Washington, D.C.: National Academy of Science, 1988.

*The Continuing Growth of Hunger, Homelessness and Poverty in America's Cities — 1987: A 26-City Survey.* Washington, D.C.: United States Conference of Mayors, 1987.

Crosbie, Michael J. *Owner-Homebuilding and Improvement in the United States: An Inquiry into its Nature and Search for Avenue of Greater Architect Participation.* Washington, D.C.: Catholic University of Maryland, 1983.

A Decent Place to Live: The Report of the National Housing Task Force. Washington, D.C.: The National Housing Task Force, March 1988.

Erickson, Jon, and Charles Wilhelm, ed. Housing the Homeless. Rutgers, N.J.: Center for Urban Policy Research, 1986.

"Essays on Social Housing," Progressive Architecture. New York City: Volume LXV, No. 7, July 1984.

Homelessness: Critical Issues for Policy and Practice. Boston, Mass.: The Boston Foundation, 1987.

Homelessness in America — 1988: Hearing Before the Subcommittee on Housing and Community Development of the Committee on Banking, Finance, and Urban Affairs, House of Representatives. Washington, D.C.: U.S. Government Printing Office, 1988.

Housing and Homelessness. Washington, D.C.: Alliance Housing Council, National Alliance to End Homelessness. 1988.

Kuttner, Robert. "Bad Housekeeping: The housing crisis and what to do about it." The New Republic. Washington, D.C., April 25, 1988, pp. 22-25.

Mallach, Alan. Inclusionary Housing Programs: Policies and Practices. Rutgers, N.J.: Center for Urban Policy Research, 1984.

A Manual on Transitional Housing. Boston, Mass.: Women's Institute for Housing and Economic Development Inc., 1986.

Mayer, Robert, and Tillie Shuster. Developing Shelter Models for the Homeless: 3 Program Design Options. New York City: Community Service Society of New York, 1985.

Meeting America's Housing Needs: Through Rehabilitation of Existing Housing and Vacant Buildings. Washington, D.C.: The National Institute of Building Sciences, 1987.

Nenno, Mary K. Assistance for Homeless Persons: A NAHRO Resource Book for Housing and Community Development Agencies. Washington, D.C.: The National Association of Housing and Redevelopment Officials, 1988.

Nenno, Mary K., and George Colyer. New Money & New Methods: A Catalog of State and Local Initiatives in Housing and Community Development. Volumes I and II. Washington, D.C.: The National Association of Housing and Redevelopment Officials, 1986 and 1988.

Peirce, Neal R., and Carol F. Steinbach. Corrective Capitalism: The Rise of America's Community Development Corporations. New York City: The Ford Foundation, 1987.

Riordan, Teresa. "Housekeeping at HUD: Why the homeless problem could get much, much worse." Common Cause Magazine. March/April 1987, pp. 26-31.

The Scope of Social Architecture. C. Richard Hatch (ed.). New York City: Van Nostrand Reinhold Co. 1984.

Sprague, Joan Forrester. A Manual on Transitional Housing. Boston: Women's Institute for Housing and Economic Development, Inc., 1986.

Stegman, Michael A., and J. David Holden. Nonfederal Housing Programs: How States and Localities Are Responding to Federal Cutbacks in Low-Income Housing. Washington, D.C.: Urban Land Institute, 1987 (revised).

# CASE STUDIES CITY INDEX

# CASE STUDIES
# SUBJECT INDEX